Building Dioramas

CHRIS MROSKO

KALMBACH BOOKS

Kalmbach Books
21027 Crossroads Circle
Waukesha, Wisconsin 53186
www.Kalmbach.com/Books

Published in 2014

18 17 16 15 14   1 2 3 4 5

This product is a Print on Demand format of the original book published by Kalmbach Publishing Company.

ISBN: 978-0-89024-870-6
EISBN: 978-1-62700-177-9

Writing consultant: Mark Hembree
Editors: Mark Hembree, Randy Rehberg
Art Director: Tom Ford
Illustrator: Jay Smith

Unless otherwise noted, all photographs were taken by the author.

Publisher's Cataloging-In-Publication Data

Mrosko, Chris.
  Building dioramas / Chris Mrosko.

   pages : color illustrations ; cm. -- (FineScale modeler books)

   Issued also as an ebook.
   ISBN: 978-0-89024-870-6

   1. Models and modelmaking--Design and construction--Handbooks,
manuals, etc. 2. Diorama--Design and construction--Handbooks, manuals,
etc. 3. Military miniatures. I. Title. II. Series: FineScale modeler books.

TT154 .M76 2014
745.5928/2

Contents

Some 20 plus years ago, the Hong Kong model company that I had been working with launched a subsidiary in Los Angeles. It wasn't long before I began to receive telephone queries from the staff, looking for various bits of information to assist in their production of resin figures. One of those fellows introduced himself as Chris Mrosko.

I had been a lifelong model enthusiast, so I suspected that I had heard about this guy through the various modeling magazines that I subscribed to. (Remember, this was long before the Internet.) Chris spoke in an exuberant manner, acting as if we had known each other for years. Quite frankly, this rather reserved writer was not quite sure just what to think of him. However, we began a close friendship that transcended the miles that separated us.

I attended a hobby show in LA in the mid-1990s, where we were finally able to meet. It became obvious that he was a man with many friends and that his life revolved around our hobby. By this time, Chris was involved in his own model business, Warriors, with partner John Rosengrant. Together, they produced a great line of figures and accessories for a number of years until John's talented work in the movie industry required his full attention, and they sold Warriors to VLS in Missouri.

It was there that I first viewed the wall of awards that Chris had garnered over the years, and it was not a small wall! However, it was not as easy to see examples of his modeling work, as a regular clientele quickly purchased his finished models for their collections.

Chris has broad experience in our hobby at both personal and professional levels. He is a determined researcher, consummate builder, and professional producer. He is always eager to improve.

I suspect that we'll cross paths at another hobby show soon.

–Ron Volstad

Ron Volstad has lived his entire life in Alberta, Canada, and drawing has been his favorite pastime from a very young age. Entirely self-taught, Ron has illustrated more than 60 books and 200 model kit boxes. His interest in military subjects began when an uncle showed him photos and souvenirs from his service in the Calgary Highlanders.

[You can see Ron's illustration of Chris during his days in the service on page 119.]

first met Chris around 1991 at the SCAHMS California figure show. There is always an ordnance section at the show, and it was filled with a large sampling of Chris' work—showcasing his distinctive style of super-clean building and painting. His models were attracting quite a lot of attention.

Chris then moved out to California to take a job with DML/Marco Polo and for the first time began mixing his passionate love of the hobby with the business side. Our friendship continued, and when Chris wanted to expand his horizons, we both decided upon forming a company to provide the modeling world with a unique product line. That company was Warriors Scale Models, and it carved quite a niche for itself by setting new standards with an interesting range of figures and models.

Chris is the perfect choice to author this book. No one loves all facets of this hobby more than Chris or has the all-around expertise to give an insider's perspective. It's all covered here, from building and finishing dioramas to Chris' "wedgies." Chris generated the wedgie idea, and it's now a staple at model shows. Manufacturers sell them prepackaged, right out of the box, as well.

Chris is well-known for his airbrushing skills, and they are showcased here in depth. An exciting "first" for hobbyists is an introduction to casting in resin. Chris lays out the fundamentals of the process, shedding light on one of the vague mysteries of our hobby. (I'm sure this will be a dog-eared section of the book for those wishing to get into this aspect of modeling.)

This book is a must-have for beginners looking to expand their modeling skills as well as for serious hobbyists.

–John Rosengrant

A master modeler in his own right, John Rosengrant is a leader in the motion-picture field of character effects. You've seen his work in the *Terminator* series, the *Jurassic Park* series, *Aliens*, *Predator*, *Edward Scissorhands*, and *Avatar*. He is one of the founders of Legacy Effects, which completed projects for *John Carter of Mars*, *Real Steel*, and *Twilight: Breaking Dawn*. To learn more about John and his work, visit legacyefx.com.

A NOTE ABOUT THIS BOOK

Building great dioramas requires modeling skills from the ground up. If you're a woodworker, you can make your own wood frame to contain a display base. If you're making groundwork, you can make your own— from plaster, Celluclay, even wall patching compound—and cover it with dirt, sand, or artificial grasses and trees. But the model is not finished until you set it on the base and put it on a shelf or start taking it to shows. How much you want to put into any given project is up to you. I believe this book gives you the information to get your dioramas on the shelf.

–Chris Mrosko

Introduction

Dan Capuano is well known for doing dioramas on a grand scale. In this scene from the Battle of Arnhem, the action flows left to right in almost every regard. This advanced use of composition directs the viewer to the focal point at the center, and everything else feeds into it. Not every diorama has to be this complicated, but this one certainly is entertaining. *Dan Capuano*

The composition of a diorama or a vignette is the thesis, or foundational idea, of a project. Its success depends on its proof—how well your modeling gets your idea across. The strength of the project is the composition. A strong composition results in an effective display that elevates your model.

A base is an important factor in effectively displaying a model. A model without a base is boring, as is one sitting on just a plain wood plaque. Use the base to your advantage when composing your diorama and create a presentation that captures the eye.

Ideas and planning

I find modeling ideas everywhere, every day. I can be in downtown St. Louis looking at the wall of an old brick building and get ideas, **1**. I'm inspired by what I see around me, and that includes things other modelers have done. I'll see something I like and wonder if I can embellish it and make it better. Finding an idea you like is the first step in planning your diorama.

Another way to find ideas is looking through reference material. There are numerous sources for references, and with the Internet, more than ever before are dedicated to military history. Military history is fascinating to read, but for references, it's all about the photos. I have purchased books for the sake of one photograph that captured my imagination or that I needed to help tell a story. (I have a book about manhole covers. Really.)

I'm interested in tackling a diorama of the WWII battle at Arnhem, and I purchased *Kampfraum Arnhem* (*Battle Zone Arnhem*, RZM Publishing). It's huge! With 274 photos in its 308 pages, it features many full-page photos loaded with detail. This book has given me a ton of ideas on an Arnhem diorama and is in the top five of the hundreds of reference books I own.

Films are also a valuable reference source. In addition to documentaries, Hollywood productions, such as *Saving Private Ryan* and *Band of Brothers*, contain many ideas for dioramas and vignettes.

All the world's a gauge

Rather than taking an idea straight to building a model, or fitting an existing model to an idea, I first try to place the elements of a diorama together in my mind. When deciding what you want to do, and how you want to compose the scene, the most important factor is to gauge the scale and size. That's how creative ideas turn practical. I'll make sketches or take notes of what I want to do. Sometimes my plan will change in the middle. If I think something's not working, I'll change it up a little bit.

TIP: Knowing actual dimensions of an object can help you set the scale for what goes around it.

Before you start the modeling process, estimate the size and scale to know how

1 Where does an idea originate? Which came first, the wall or the Kübelwagen? In my case, it might be the wall. I made a mental note of it when I saw it in St. Louis, and, when I planned this diorama, I remembered the wall and built it to go with the model.

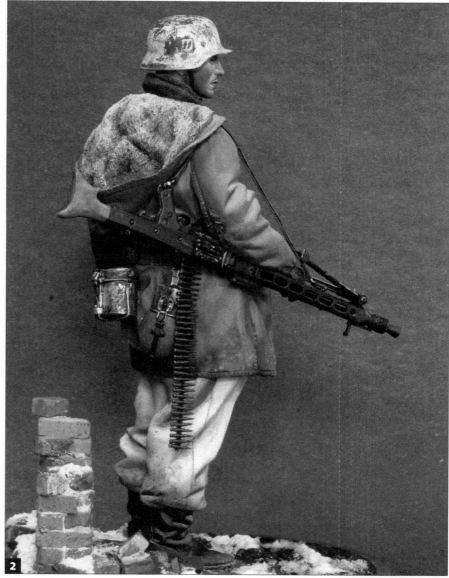

2 Here's a figure by John Rosengrant with an MG42 machine gun. The actual machine gun is 44" long, which determined the size of the figure and other elements. *John Rosengrant*

3

In September 1944, soldiers of the 60th Infantry Regiment advance into a Belgian town under the protection of a Sherman tank. You can use the height of buildings, walls, and other objects shown in a photo to help you scale the figures and surroundings in your diorama. On the front of the Sherman tank, you'll see Culin cutters, which were used to cut through the hedgerows of France.

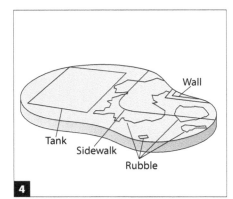

4

It's smart and less expensive to draw a plan before buying materials. A full-size sketch can help you determine materials as well as whether you'll have enough of everything—including space for your models and figures.

big you want to go and the space you need. Sure, I could go back downtown and measure that old brick wall, but I can save myself that trip too. If I positively know the size of something, like a standard brick, I can use that to measure out how big a wall I need.

Once, I watched John Rosengrant sculpt a figure. He knew the size of an MG42 machine gun, and, looking at a picture of a German soldier standing next to it, we decided this guy had to be about 6' 3" or 6' 4" with a build like Max Schmelling. By knowing its size, he used that machine gun to set the scale, **2**.

If you have a reference photo of a Sherman tank, and you like the surroundings and want to do something similar, use the

scale in the photo and transfer it to your diorama, **3**.

Sketch it out

Using your tentative shape and dimensions, cut a piece of Styrofoam, plywood, or foam core to represent your base. Use that piece as a template on which to lay out the elements of your diorama. (I'll cut a palette-shaped base out of foam core.) Lay any completed (or partially completed) pieces on the base and sketch in other details around them to visualize the composition of your diorama. This makes it easy to change things around while you are still in the planning stage, **4**. Do this before you buy an expensive decorative frame or a nice plaque or wooden base.

5

Marcus Nicholls, courtesy of Tamiya Model Magazine International

6

You can sculpt groundwork and build buildings, but what really brings a diorama to life are the mundane, everyday items you would expect to see in a natural setting. Here, Mirko Bayerl of Värmdö, Sweden, has built a European farmhouse with features that make a house a home, from the chimney with do-it-yourself repairs to the rough-hewn bench by the door. The half door adds a rural touch; it lets fresh air in and keeps chickens and goats out. A Schwimmwagen in the garage lends a bit of irony that says *occupation*. *Mirko Bayerl/Toni Canfora*

Minimal groundwork supports this masterful figure by Carlos Startin of Leicester, England. The good-looking base is not so complicated that it distracts from the figure. A display this size still gives you plenty to do.

Think it through before you go spend a bunch of money on materials. This way, you know at the start whether your composition will work.

I favor bases no bigger than 18" x 18". For me, it's hard to put as much heart and detail into something bigger than that. If you have an 8' x 8' diorama on a big sheet of plywood, you're going to have multiple focal points and story lines—and you're going to take 100 years to complete it!

I'll spend as much time as it takes to complete a diorama. But if I'm doing one with one vehicle and three or four figures and some groundwork, a few months is long enough for me to plan, build, and finish a diorama of that size.

To establish the size and scope of a diorama, determine the level of detail you want to undertake. If you have a ruined building, are you going to show something as miniscule as a push-button light switch? Showing a picture hanging from one of the standing walls is one level of detail; having a shard of broken glass in the picture frame takes it to another level.

You also have to consider painting and weathering the pieces. Will you give a piece of wrought iron a patina finish or paint it black?

LAYOUT, COMPOSITION, AND SHEPERD PAINE

From the time I decided I wanted to do this book, I knew it would have to include a special mention of Sheperd Paine. There's no single artist more famous among modelers. He, more than anyone, is the reason I'm able to present this book—and that I build models at all.

Shep's book, *How to Build Dioramas*, changed my life. He was the first to demonstrate the classic ideas of layout and composition to modelers. As he wrote: "*Composition* is determining the overall design of the diorama, while *layout* is arranging various parts to fit that design."

To this day, I apply the principles of building dioramas I learned from him in that book, especially in being mindful of the composition as I arrange its elements—those "various parts"—to establish sight lines that carry the viewer's eyes throughout the scene.

As Shep described it, the viewer sees a diorama in three stages—overall, then in a little more detail, and, finally, down to the individual elements of the diorama. How this process proceeds

determines whether the viewer understands the "story" you're trying to tell.

The viewer will likely "read" your diorama from left to right because that's how the eye is conditioned, at first with a glance, and then by retracing his steps and stopping at the right side. There, where the eye stops, is the "hot spot" in the diorama. How you align individual elements—a gun barrel pointing back toward the center, or figures looking that way—can further direct the viewer's eye.

It is at this point that you hope the viewer has been drawn into your work, looking more closely at the modeling—the figure painting, the vehicles, the expressions on the figures' faces—and seamlessly regarding the surroundings—terrain, vegetation, or an urban setting—to understand the story it tells.

That's my goal with any display or diorama—to draw the viewer through the scene to sense the moment and understand what I'm trying to depict. That I learned from Shep, still a creative force behind my dioramas.

Doug Lee is a modeler who pours an awful lot into a diorama. These two photos are of the same diorama. It was too big for me to get one good picture of the entire thing!

The peaceful farmhouse shown in photo 5 is now surrounded by action. Here, Mirko Bayerl added more farmyard features—tools, geese, a feed cart—but the German soldiers and the tank have become the focus. Each figure is engaged in a believable action. And, speaking of focus, note how the figures on the far left and far right direct your eye toward the center. That is no accident, but effective composition at work. *Mirko Bayerl/Toni Canfora*

9

An unusual pose or setting based on an image can gain credence if the image is included in the display, such as on this diorama built by Robert Döpp, of Hemmingen, Germany. *Robert Döpp*

10

Pretty as a picture—but surprising as a model. Sepia tones evoke a historical portrait, but the subject and surroundings are truly 3-D in this wall mount by the late Dieter Mattingly.

A cat wandering around in the scene and many other little things add life to a display, **5**. That's when those arcane reference books on architecture, interior finishes, and manhole covers come in handy.

When building a diorama, I usually start with a vehicle, but something might come along and convince me to go in another direction. Start small. If you bite off a bigger diorama than you can chew, the modeling may be no fun at all. It can become more work than you want to get into and burn you out, so keep your diorama small enough that you enjoy building it through the entire process, **6**.

Figures and composition

Figures relate or show the fidelity of scale, but they have to be done well to contribute. A true diorama has a focal point—not just 30 figures on a base standing around—and shows a slice of life. The figures direct the focus and make the scene come alive.

Korean modeler Douglas Lee can do an 18" x 18" diorama with a slew of figures.

His dioramas are dynamic with multiple focal points, **7**.

Is there a limit to how many figures to include? Well, two to five figures make a vignette. More than that, you're looking at a pretty good-sized diorama. In a military setting, there may be a group of soldiers who happen to be standing around. But for the purpose of display, you want to get rid of the ones that are not essential.

If you have a tank and crew, you can have one soldier standing on the tank, pointing forward, and talking to another soldier hanging out of the hatch. Don't let them just stand there, **8**.

In composing a scene where some soldiers are changing a flat tire on a jeep, how many does it really take? It's a one- or two-person job (not counting buddies who want to stand around and crack wise).

Now, think about what the soldiers were doing before the jeep got the flat. Thinking creatively and imagining a story can help you decide what to put in or around that jeep. Do you want to

add mud? Not if you're in the desert. Do you want it to be dusty? It could be, but maybe not in a rainy climate. This should all be in your mind before you start modeling.

In another scenario, let's say the jeep is full of airmen from a bomber that just landed. You've got eight or nine guys piled into the jeep, stacked on top of each other. In this scene, your composition is going vertical, and the diorama can even fit on a smaller base.

There are numerous ways to compose with the same models and figures. Imagining and thinking things through are among the most important elements of composition. Use your references and photos. You'll see a lot of interesting stuff out there, and if you choose a really different scene, you might want to display the photo with it. That way, people will understand what you're trying to do, **9**.

Sometimes you can even make a model display look like a picture itself, by putting the model in a frame where the image is a three-dimensional object, **10**.

Steve Hustad's 1/72 scale diorama combines figures, an artfully damaged Junkers Ju 52, and groundwork featuring a Celluclay base covered with Verlinden static grass, Woodland Scenics scrub brush, and Hudson & Allen snow mixed with Verlinden thermoplastic microballoons. The sum of these elements is the story: it's late winter in Luxembourg and the war is not going well for the Germans.

"The Last Supper" shows German soldiers pausing for a quick meal before bugging out of Normandy. As the first diorama I ever sold, it's not bad. Since then, my composition (and photography) has improved in terms of focus. For instance, the two soldiers around the corner of the church (at right) contribute little to the scene.

You can even build a narrative with just one model. For instance, a crashed airplane tells its own story, **11**.

One of my first serious dioramas (and the first one I ever sold) was called "The Last Supper." Although there's a fair amount of action in it, and it's focused, it is not as simple and direct as the dioramas I do now, **12**.

Natural environment— elements in their element

In a good composition, groundwork, foliage, models, and figures all have to agree. If you're going to do a diorama of the British Special Air Services on patrol in North Africa, you want desert terrain, figures in desert garb, vehicles correctly painted and marked for the time and locale, and a pose that's in line with all the elements, **13**.

If you are modeling an American tanker at the Battle of the Bulge, even though he may not be on the ground in the elements, he should be muddy if he's on the tank, **14**. Don't pose a clean, dry figure on the tank. Show the context; do a continuity check. How did the soldier get on the tank? If he climbed up on that tank, add a little grime to support the story. Show the lead-up to the final results.

Research and imagine. Lean on your visual references. If you have an Afrika Korps theme, look at a variety of desert scenes, not just PzKpfw IIs in Africa. Read books on the Afrika Korps and desert warfare, and study the terrain. Then you can set the scene of your diorama.

You could come up with a nice, sandy setting, but not necessarily a pristine one or one at an oasis. Look at your resources and imagine where the setting is going to be and decide how you're going to create it.

But don't get so hung up on one reference or photo that it limits you. Everything you use doesn't have to be from the same photograph. You can add elements from other sources as well. Beg, borrow, and steal, **15**.

You can add a lot of life to even a small scene. Whether it's a bit of stonework and a bridge, a little lizard hiding behind a rock, or a dog in the yard, incorporate it! These small details add up. Imagine the place, look around, and visualize what you see. Add little touches of ordinary life to make

John Rosengrant's SAS patrol conveys desert from the sandy and scrubby groundwork to the soldiers' keffiyehs, an adoption of local garb to protect the head and neck from sunburn. Every detail contributes to set the scene and tell the story. *John Rosengrant*

This is an example of an accurately imagined scene. Many details place John Rosengrant's diorama at the Battle of the Bulge, including the snow on the ground, the Sherman Jumbo tank fitted with "grousers" on the track (extensions to reduce ground pressure in muddy conditions), and the European ruins behind the scene. On the tank, the muddy footprints left by the soldier standing next to the turret further animate the scene. There are a lot of figures to manage in this diorama, but John does a great job of engaging all of them in credible actions: the dogfaces on the left cutting up and killing time, while the tank commander studies the map.

15

This compact display of a Hungarian freedom fighter combines ideas and symbols from several accounts of the 1956 Hungarian Revolt: János Mész, known as "John with the Wooden Leg"; the Hungarian flag (made from lead foil) with the Communist Rákosi coat of arms cut out; revolutionary street painting; and, on the ground, makings for a Molotov cocktail, a valuable weapon against Soviet tanks in the streets.

16

A sense of place is important for any diorama but especially for aircraft displays. An airplane may not leave as much room for surroundings unless the diorama is oversized. But the runway alone can tell a lot. Here, the runway, with its snowy, slushy groundwork, coupled with the Bf 109's winter camouflage, indicates that the setting is the Eastern Front.

the scene more interesting, and you'll also have more fun with your project.

Aircraft

Whether in a vignette or a full-blown diorama, displaying airplanes is a whole different game than is displaying ground vehicles. But the same basic principles of composition and layout apply. You don't want to just center the plane on a totally square base or a completely round one. To plan your diorama, imagine the setting and what the surroundings should be. Then set a scene and incorporate the elements that describe its time and place.

Unless an aircraft is posed in flight, it has to be on a base, and unless it crashed during a flight, an aircraft on the ground is going to be on a runway. Is the runway concrete? Coral? Grass? The type of runway often tells the story, **16**. One possibility is to start with an irregularly shaped base and place the airplane there with part of the tarmac or Marsden matting (also known as PSP, or perforated steel planking). Find some sources, do your research, and have at it.

I've always thought it would be great to model three or four B-17s taxiing for takeoff, and maybe add a few P-51 or P-47 fighters nearby. Well, you could have all those models in relatively close proximity, but really, to be accurate, that scene would have to be on a massive base. Modeling a 3- or 4-square-foot base might not be practical.

An airplane doesn't have to be very big to trigger an ambitious diorama, **17**. Steve Hustad does terrific work in 1/72 scale—models about half the scale of the ones I usually do—and even in that smaller scale, the dioramas are still fairly large.

With larger planes, you'll need a pretty big base. Estimate the size before you start, and you may want to reconsider. A man's got to know his limitations.

But those practical considerations can often lead to imaginative solutions. What can you do to develop a concept and tell a story?

Using artistic license

For modelers, artistic license means stretching the truth, exaggerating or abbreviating something to get an idea across. Most modelers take liberties or embellish for the sake of telling the

17 In 1/72 scale, Steve Hustad's diorama is still sizable. It features a good size plane that requires space around it to tell this particular story. Steve's modeling of the rocks and water represents a lot of work above and beyond the building of the basic kit and provides dramatic results.

18 A shadow box goes even further than sight lines and suggestion to focus the viewer's attention. Dave Browne of Toronto won a first-place award at the prestigious Military Miniatures Society of Illinois' annual show in 2009 with this tribute to Abraham Lincoln's 200th birthday in 1/35 scale. The shadow box recreates the studio of Daniel Chester French, whose famous sculpture is in the Lincoln Memorial. Dave imagined this scene after visiting the sculptor's studio and studying photos.

At first glance, this model might be another fearsome German self-propelled gun. But wait. What is that thing? It's huge! It's a paper panzer, an experimental design never produced. If you build something like this, you can take some liberties with the uniforms and locale since it's a fictional scenario, what modelers like to call "what if." Greg Cihlar's 1/35 scale diorama "1946" is an impressive fabrication featuring a hypothetical vehicle, 12.8cm PaK 44 Waffentrager, a resin kit by Cromwell Models.

This Royal Enfield 1942 WD/RE 125cc Airborne motorcycle, "The Flying Flea," is scratch-built in 1/9 scale by Alex De Leon, along with the hand-laid bricks and fire hydrant. Alex has paid attention to the layout of the base by not parking the bike perpendicular to the curb or edges of the base. He uses color modulation and other techniques. Here, paint implies light—look at the top of the hydrant and the motorcycle's gas tank. *Alex De Leon*

story, in small and sometimes in big ways.

For instance, I have a vignette idea for a POW camp that shows a survivor on the inside, up against the wires, both hands on the wire and leaning forward, looking out. On the other side of the fence is an American soldier, looking in. But to do the scene right, they can't be that close together. You have to allow more space than you actually need. You have to embellish the setting—the fencing and scenery—because if you don't, it's just going to look like two guys standing on either side of a barbed wire fence. You need more than that around them.

You could work from a different focal point or perspective and change the point of view. Imagine yourself as the American soldier, and it's you looking in and the prisoner is looking back at you. Now you have a point of view, a picture. You could put that figure in a small shadow box and use forced perspective

21

Even when the colors are known and standardized (such as the Federal Standard, or FS, numbers listed here) and the subject is the same, the variables of light, film, exposure, and mixing paint in the field can conspire to confuse. All these F-4 Phantoms wear the same Southeast Asia scheme: FS34102 medium green, FS34079 dark green, FS30219 dark tan, and FS36622 camouflage gray—but you couldn't prove it with these photos.

behind and maybe show the front of a building.

TIP: By using a shadow box, you can limit the view of a scene and direct the viewer's eye more exactly.

A shadow box directs viewers to a visual space that wouldn't be as perceptible in an open display, **18**. They will be more likely to see what you want them to because you are controlling the space around the subject.

About those bothersome facts

Artistic license is one thing, but unless your intent is to amuse, many people expect to see historical accuracy when modeling armor, aircraft, ships, figure uniforms, and other subjects.

Ron Volstad, who has drawn a lot of box art for major model manufacturers, told me that every time he finishes a piece, he thinks he's done every bit of research in the world. But, he says, "Just wait. Wait until I get this done. There's

going to be somebody that comes up with a photograph to prove me wrong. It happens every time."

Some modelers want to be as correct about everything as possible. Still, there are ways to free yourself from the tyranny of the exactness of the facts.

For example, you could model the experimental vehicles called *paper panzers* that the Germans were developing at the end of WWII but never produced. In this case, you can do whatever you want

22

Douglas Lee's "Lord of Cyrenica" diorama is a clear demonstration of the "rule of thirds," front to back, side to side, and top to bottom. Consider front to back: one horseman, the tank, and two horsemen at the far side. You get the same order of subject when you view it from side to side. The same order persists from the bottom up as you view the base, the groundwork, and the models. From every angle, the thirds are nearly equally divided. By adding the dog, the number of subjects (five) is an odd number, which is another basic tenet of artistic design.

23

This base demonstrates our basic rules. Note how nothing is parallel nor perpendicular to the edges of the base, and neither the model nor the other elements are parallel to each other. The groundwork isn't level, either. In nearly every aspect, symmetry has been avoided.

INTEREST IN DIORAMAS

There's no single artist more famous among modelers than Sheperd Paine. If not for Shep, a lot of us would be totally lost today. Shep was one of the first modelers who really grasped and demonstrated the classic ideas of layout and composition.

If not for his diorama tips packed in Monogram kit boxes years ago, it would be a whole different world of modeling today. Some of us had just started building models, but when we got those little pamphlets in the kits, we wanted to build dioramas.

I wanted to do figures and bases and groundwork. Those little pamphlets alone inspired me to want to be a better modeler, to be able to display my work, and maybe one day show Shep Paine what an inspiration he had been to me.

with the paint schemes and surroundings since the paper panzer didn't exist—it's all make-believe, **19**.

Modelers like to go overboard building the Maus (a gigantic experimental German tank) and have a ball—the vehicle also never went into production. You can pretend it did, have a lot of fun building it, and not worry about portraying every factual detail!

One drawback with all the prototype information now available is that recently accessible photos and other research have proved a lot of people's models wrong. (It's now hard to get away with anything!)

On the other hand, artistic modelers who are also master painters may build armor models, for example, but they apply classic painting principles, color modulation and such, and don't worry so much about someone calling them on an inaccuracy. They can work outside those confines to express themselves with their painting and shading and weathering techniques, **20**.

Beware of photographic evidence

Photographic references can be tricky and variable. World War II photos are mostly black-and-white, and variables include film exposure, shadows and sunlight, and natural surroundings. Color photos can

24 There's not much beside the figure on this base, but there are still enough details to set time and place and provide a context for the figure.

25 You don't have to make every display base a masterpiece. Nothing wrong with a simple base—but model something that gives the figure a place and a reason to be there.

also be affected by the same variables and the film developing process, **21**.

Another factor that can skew the color in a photo is the actual color of the vehicles. If a vehicle was painted in the field, its color could vary from a vehicle that was painted in the factory. Conditions in the field were less controlled. Paint could be mixed in 50-gallon drums or thinned with diesel or gasoline, which would change the color.

Rules for effective design

Rule 1: Avoid centering models. This is the first rule of laying out a diorama. You don't want to limit your usable space for reinforcing or emphasizing your main model, whether it's adding buildings, other vehicles, figures, animals, whatever. When you have a model dead center, you've killed the area around it.

Another rule, the "rule of thirds," is a basic compositional philosophy you can easily apply. For example, I like to have a model offset on the base, occupying about one third of the base, and then I have two thirds of subordinate space I can use for sidewalks or buildings to make a little bit of a scene and create a tableau, **22**.

Even if you're using a round base, you can place your model on a third of the base and not dead center. This gives you space to show off groundwork, a street section, or part of a wall. You can still use your creativity and imagination to add that Wow Factor. Do something with that extra area, **23**.

It disappoints me when modelers take a 54mm (2⅛") figure, which ought to go on a base about 2" x 2" x 2," and put it on a smaller pedestal with just a

smudge of dirt under its feet. That's fine if you want nothing but the figure, but it doesn't leave room for anything else. Show a little background. Give that figure a little room to breathe and come to life, **24**.

As always, there are exceptions—you don't always have to have a vehicle running from corner to corner on a base. In some scenes, you can show a vehicle parallel or perpendicular to the edges of the base, or you can center a model, and it can look good, especially ships, trains, or a half-track pulling an artillery piece. But if you can, offset it slightly to get a little more use out of the base. Give yourself more room for a sidewalk or other little things you can add to bring life to the scene. There's a lot you can add without upstaging or overpowering the subject, **25**.

This diorama features excellent masonry and a good-looking model—but you notice the soldiers first. As soon as figures are out of the vehicle, especially if they are dramatically posed, they become the focal point.

Even in a scene as detailed as Dan Capuano's Arnhem diorama, notice how he uses elements of the scene to focus the action and redirect the viewer back to the focal point, the soldiers in the center: the angles of the streetcar and jeep, the soldiers pointing in the background, and even the wrought-iron railing. *Dan Capuano*

28

Defining points of view helps point the way. Providing distinct details from well-defined aspects adds variety and interest, even with a small display.

Eyepath and visual attraction

If you have a model on a base with a figure standing by it, the first thing people will look at is the figure. But you first need to decide if the figure is what you want them to focus on.

If you model an airplane with a figure in the cockpit, or a vehicle with a figure or two in it, people will look at the model first and then the figure. But if the figure's on the outside of the model, people see it first, **26**.

Decide ahead of time what you want people to focus on, and then compose your elements to support the focal point. But don't add so much that it detracts from your main focal point. Whatever secondary elements you add, you want them to point back to the main subject. For example, if you build a tank diorama, you place an abandoned vehicle in the background. You don't want to place it all the way to the right or to the left, as this pulls your eyes away from the main sight lines. You want that secondary item in your direct vision, in your line of sight but directing your eyes toward the main subject or focal point, **27**.

Often, viewers will go and look at the other side of a model just to see if there's something hiding there. If you put a model on a turnstile or a Lazy Susan, or in a diorama, people are more inclined to look at all of it to see if it has that Wow Factor.

If you're using a round base, you can turn the diorama, so you need to have more than one way draw attention to the focal point or establish different focal points, **28**. It's a different design approach knowing that a model is going to be seen from 360 degrees, which is why I like using round bases. Depending on your vantage point, you're going to see things in a different order, or you'll see more as you move from the primary model to secondary ones. I'll add entertaining details that keep viewers engaged from several different views. Many modelers enjoy playing *Where's Waldo?* by hiding extra objects in a diorama, which can be cute or funny, but which shouldn't be a distraction and take away from the diorama's subject.

There are several ways to use figures to establish or induce an eyepath. Instead of placing them single file or all bunched

up, you can show them indirectly pointing the way to the focal point of a display, **29**. A few soldiers could be walking in front of a tank holding their rifles, and your eyes follow the rifles to the tank. Another figure could be sitting on the tank scraping mud from the soles of his boots, and your eyes might go from there to a tank commander hanging out of the turret smoking a pipe, eating a sandwich, or taking a drink from his canteen. All these elements direct the viewer, and you need to determine the order in which viewers will see them.

Using space

You can show a lot in a small diorama, but you have to carefully plan the composition ahead of time. You don't always have to build a big horizontal base. Remember, you can always build up.

You don't want to keep too much space around the model, unless you want to express vastness, such as a desert, but that's hard to get across with just one stretch of sand.

In an urban setting, space becomes a more critical factor. You have to be more mindful of all the viewing angles, sight

29 John Rosengrant's diorama incorporates a variety of figures. The positioning and posing of the figures lets the viewer set the point of view.

30 I'm planning how to use this spare building section, and I sketched an idea right on the part. It helps to draw it up before you cut it up.

lines, and tighter confines. You'll most likely want to use up every bit of space that you have on an urban diorama. You don't want to leave any dead space.

If you have to model a street intersection, do you just want to show one corner of a building and the vehicle? No, you would be better off showing two or three corners of an intersection, angled on the base so you have smaller sections, but the vehicle can be the center of attention. It's more complete and fills up more space.

When you design streets, they don't have to form a perfect, equilateral +. They can be angled, as many city streets are. You can also vary the presentation of the buildings, **30**. They don't all have to be the same size. You can have a large part of one building and a smaller portion of another. This is how you create an eye-path. Think of it as a wedge or an arrow pointing the way to the focal point.

In your diorama, you place a tank in an intersection, with buildings on three corners. They don't have to be large sections of buildings, just enough to give the idea that this tank is stopped in the middle of an intersection. This way, the flow, or eye-path, comes from outside into the display.

In the planning stages, you can mock up cardboard buildings and position them on the base. Take a marker and draw any features you want on the buildings—win-

dows, battle damage, whatever. If the buildings are too big, you can just cut them down. You can build up your streets, outlining the path of the streets or sidewalks, which gives you room to play with the composition including the angles you want and how you want to pose vehicles. If a tank is your subject, you can balance it out with smaller vehicles such as an abandoned cart, a tractor, a shot-up car, an abandoned jeep, or a Kübelwagen.

Don't use a base that is too small for the model. If you're displaying a tank, and the barrel overhangs the edge of the base, that's OK, no problem. But I've never liked when the tank itself hangs off the edge of a base—unless you're using that composition to tell a story. For example, in one diorama, I saw a tank posed partially on the base, and the base's edge was all chewed up as if the tank had just crawled up onto it. It defied the rules of symmetry and composition, but it was still entertaining. Things like that sometimes work. Just plan it out ahead of time.

Implying space

Much of the magic of a display depends on being able to effectively imply space—suggesting something that isn't actually there. For instance, two figures could look out at something in the distance or look into a building or a cave, even though the

whole building or cave is not part of the base.

But you can't just have two soldiers looking at an empty hole in the ground. If you were to do a shadow box, you could have one soldier in a tunnel and another soldier deeper in, maybe on his knees, seeming to peer around a corner, which would imply a greater depth than the actual physical space available on the diorama base. Another way to imply space is to show models in a sectional view, obviously parts of a greater whole, **31**.

Magic tricks

Along with everything you can accomplish with composition, there are amazing innovations people come up with to create unique displays. Many modelers still recall Lynn Rowley's shadow box that showed a midair collision between a B-17F and a Bf 109G, which he showed at the IPMS Nationals in Virginia Beach, Va., in 1996. Through forced perspective, placing the 1/72 scale bomber in the background and the 1/48 scale fighter in the foreground, Lynn made it look as if the 109 was disintegrating, **32**.

I looked and looked at the shadow box, and finally Lynn said, "Well, did you figure out how I got all those pieces in the air?" He explained that the various pieces were glued to separate sheets of clear acetate, and a mirror added depth to the scene.

This diorama is an example of how to imply space. Obviously, there is no cellar, and the illusion of an underground area is well executed, with the German soldiers posed walking up stairs. The imagination makes up the remainder of the unseen cellar. The American soldier pointing his BAR directs your eye to the surrendering Germans.

Famous diorama, famous photo: Lynn Rowley created a shadow-box display based on a photo taken after a Bf 109G German fighter collided with the B-17 *All American* and nearly severed the tail from the bomber. In this forced perspective, pieces of the disintegrating fighter are attached to sheets of clear acetate at various depths inside the box. The B-17 in the background is 1/72 scale, modified to replicate the damage of the actual plane. Former *FineScale Modeler* Senior Editor Paul Boyer photographed the model; the other shot is a U.S. Air Force photo taken by a P-51 pilot escorting the bomber back to England, where it landed safely.

Finishing the diorama

So how do you know when a diorama is finished? You've accomplished the goals you set forth. You've used the model, figures, and base that you wanted. You've added little details that help set the scene. You've completed the right level of appropriate weathering for the time, place, climate, and season. The diorama is everything that you wanted. You just know when it's done.

But don't be surprised if you're at a club meeting or a show, and somebody says, "Hey, where's this?" and you realize you forgot something. It happens. You can't think of everything. It's impossible.

That's why it's always good to have other people look at your diorama while it's in progress. They'll see things that you don't see or enhance an idea. I've made numerous changes based on people's comments. Share your work, let others see it, and listen to their comments.

Groundwork

It takes time and energy to build a good-looking base. A piece of plywood is at the bottom of this one. Layers of Apoxie Sculpt are on top of that, followed by a mix of groundwork, plastic, and resin castings. From front to back, you can see white molded-plastic cobblestone, taffy-colored resin sidewalk, gravel and real dirt, random premade rubble, and resin-cast building ruins. I sculpted the steps with Apoxie Sculpt.

In his seminal modeling book *How to Build Dioramas*, Sheperd Paine urged modelers who spend "inordinate" amounts of time on their models to devote more time and energy to the bases on which they are displayed.

"The base forms the frame for your diorama picture," he wrote, "and just as you would not put a Rembrandt in a dime-store frame, neither should you put your model on a hunk of scrap lumber."

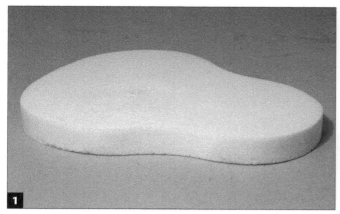

1 Many of my dioramas start with one of these palette- or kidney-shaped bases. You can cut one out of balsa foam, Styrofoam, foam core, or other light, easy-to-cut materials.

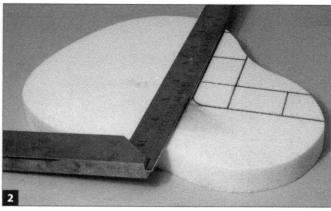

2 I have the models and the scene I want to build worked out in my mind. Sketching the layout is the first step toward realizing the diorama's composition.

3 Using a straightedge, I scribe sidewalk blocks on thick styrene. They don't have to be exactly the same, and if one gets chipped a little, it's OK—these are old sidewalks.

4 Sanding turns smooth styrene into rough concrete. A strip of styrene replicates the curb. Later, this piece will serve as a master for resin-casting additional pieces.

With convincing groundwork, that "frame" actually becomes part of the picture. You need to make sure the groundwork fits the location and time of where the story takes place. Photo research can help you establish these things. Learning what is possible—and looks good—is important in getting your story across.

The elements of a diorama are the models, figures, buildings, and other artifacts on a given display base. To display your modeling on a shining slab of Lucite is one thing. To incorporate groundwork in your display is to place your model in a natural setting, whether it is an asphalt road, a dusty prairie, a muddy trench, or a quaint cobblestone street—or desert, savanna, or mountain pass. That's what makes a display believable.

All the ingredients of a diorama base are important: the foundation, the groundwork, and different terrains the

groundwork can represent. I'll describe several examples, starting at the bottom and working our way up.

In the examples, you'll see a few desert scenes mixed in with a preponderance of urban scenes. While the settings may appear similar, the dioramas show a variety of groundwork techniques. Beginning with World War II, fighting in urban areas became more prevalent. I enjoy the challenge of placing vehicles in these settings.

World War II street scene

Many modelers focus on World War II subjects. Although color photography from that conflict is relatively rare, reference photographs are plentiful. And in the case of European street scenes, present-day photography and some interpretation can yield plenty of relevant information.

I often use the same base as the foundation of my work, a kidney- or palette-

shaped base, **1**. I like the irregular shape because it is less restrictive than a square or rectangle and allows variety and flexibility in the composition of a scene. Depending on the orientation of the base, it can accommodate different models and different compositions.

I cut the foundation from a 1"-thick slab of balsa foam, but you could cut a similar shape from Styrofoam or another material. Whatever material you choose for the foundation, it should be water-repellent or sealed to resist water, so it doesn't soak up liquid from the groundwork materials or paint.

On the foundation, I sketched in an outline of my scene. I started by using a carpenter's square to draw a street corner, **2**. This allows me to orient thick styrene pieces and scribe them into blocks of sidewalk pavement, **3**. The blocks don't have to be exactly the same since they're not on real sidewalks.

5

I always check the composition as major pieces become available. While the vehicle, a Tasca 1/35 scale Luchs, will remain the same size, I could change the size and shape of the sidewalk.

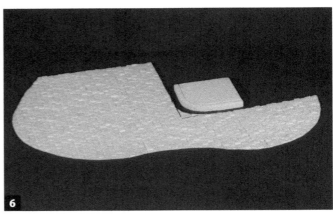

6

Verlinden and other companies mold thin plastic sheets of 1/35 scale cobblestone that are easy to install. (It sure beats laying your own bricks!)

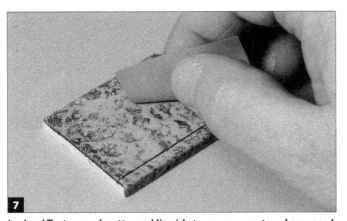

7

I mixed Testors red putty and liquid styrene cement and smeared the goop on this sidewalk block, roughing it up with an old brush, letting it dry, and then sanding down the high spots.

8

After texturing the rest of the sidewalk and cutting the cobblestone sheet to the shape of the base, I glued everything down and started to strew rubble around.

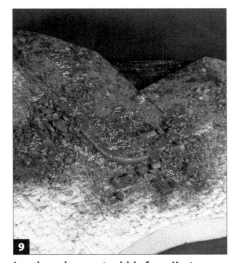

9

I anchored precast rubble from Kurton Products with thin super glue. (White glue would cover up too much.) For variety, I airbrushed the rubble red brown and hand-painted some different shades. Then I dry-brushed on a light gray, mortar/plaster tone.

After sanding the styrene block to impart a stone texture, I wrapped a styrene strip around the edge to replicate a curb, **4**. Other sidewalk segments are made the same way. Later on, I'll use this piece as a master to make a mold for casting sidewalk segments in resin to use on future dioramas.

Fitting the pieces

Before continuing, I test-fit the major elements of the scene, **5**. If I didn't like how things were shaping up at this point, I could adjust the sidewalk, or reposition the tank, but I couldn't do much about its shape or size.

Satisfied with the sidewalk's placement, I needed a street to go with it. Some modelers go to a lot of trouble to model cobblestone by scribing wet plaster or even laying individual stones. However, several manufacturers make sheets of plastic cobblestone, and for me, this is

the way to go, **6**. You can cut it to shape and simply glue it down. Using a sheet of Verlinden cobblestone, I thinned it with a belt sander so the sidewalk would be higher than the cobblestones. Then I cut it around the sidewalk and fit it to the base.

With the placement of the sidewalk confirmed, I was ready to work some more on its texture, **7**. I covered the styrene, one block at a time, with a mix of Testors red putty and Testors liquid cement. While this goop was still wet, I stippled it with a broad, stiff brush to rough it up. After the mixture dried, I sanded it to knock off the high spots.

I fit and glued the pieces in place, **8**. In the space framed by the sidewalk (the small black wedge seen in the photo), I'll add a ruined corner of a building. In this photo, you can also see some rubble begin to appear around the sidewalk.

Now it was time to add some more, **9**. I used premade rubble by Kurton Products,

LEARNING FROM OTHERS

In my youth, a trip to a local hobby shop (the Grenadier Shop in Decatur, Ill.) really opened my eyes to the possibilities of dioramas. Dave Mosser was doing things I'd never seen a modeler do before. His work featured incredible details. I mean, who puts hobnails on the boots of 1/35 scale soldiers!

I learned from many other people as well. A fellow named Brian Stewart put so much detail into small areas. If he painted a Napoleonic figure, he'd scratchbuild a whole scene to go with it. The figure was the main story, but sometimes his groundwork and base stole the show. John Rosengrant, a brilliant special-effects guy, used real materials, such as plants and dirt, to present the most authentic look. From Dieter Mattingly, I probably learned more how-to, hands-on techniques than from anyone else. And of course, I wouldn't be writing this book if it weren't for Shep Paine. Those were the mentors who shaped me and put my feet on this path.

I wanted to do something unique to make my mark, too, and all these years later, I can say that people recognize my work. I guess it's because I realized early on that groundwork is as essential as anything else you build.

10

Dressed in late-war three-color camouflage, a finished Luchs tank rolls past layers of carefully constructed rubble. The building corner is a Custom Dioramics piece that I modified for this scene.

11

Adding a mound to this groundwork meant articulating the suspension of the Marder to match. I applied slow-setting liquid styrene cement to attach the suspension and road wheels, set it in place, and let the glue dry with the model in that position. After the glue dried, I installed the tracks.

but you could use almost anything—even kitty litter (just make sure you take out the blue chips, a dead giveaway). Some modelers use white glue to anchor a mess like this, but I prefer super glue. It doesn't cling and string like white glue, which leaves the bricks and chips in sharper relief instead of smoothing them out.

After the rubble was in place, I painted it. I airbrushed the base color on the cobblestones and rubble, which was mostly Tamiya red brown (XF-64). Then I brush-painted the bricks with more Tamiya paints: hull red (XF-9), flat brown (XF-10), and Japanese army gray (XF-14). To finish, I dry-brushed the edges with a 70:30 mix of gray and white, respectively.

The rubble-painting process consisted of a lot of little steps. I just kept stacking up the rubble and applying paint until the base was done.

I painted the bricks in the ruined wall the same color as those lying on the street since they're the same bricks! Touches of white, tinted with a little flesh, replicated mortar on the top of some of the bricks. I gave the bottom of the wall a dark gray wash and highlighted it by dry-brushing on a lighter shade of gray. Finally, using a Winsor & Newton brush and a mix of 70 percent Indian red, 20 percent yellow

ochre, and 10 percent titanium white, I dry-brushed the bricks.

With the groundwork complete, I placed the tank on the base, **10**.

World War II urban scene

I wanted to create a scene in which I could pose a Tamiya 1/35 scale model of the Marder III/M tank destroyer, a late-war vehicle, with a figure from Warriors. The

12

I used a Trakz conversion set to convert Tamiya's 1/35 scale T-55 to a Tiran 5, an Israeli-modified T-55. I had an urban setting in mind to show the tank in Lebanese service.

suspension, so it would fit the ground from front to back and on both sides of the vehicle. On this model, that meant tacking the suspension in place with slow-setting liquid styrene cement, setting the vehicle in place, and then letting the glue set with the suspension in that position.

Contemporary Beirut street

A modern street or highway scene is probably less complicated than one from the 1940s. There would be no cobblestones, no nearby brick-and-mortar stoops, and no lampposts with wrought-iron adornment. For a contemporary Beirut street scene, I constructed the "base" model of a modern setting. Of course, you can add onto a scene like this by adding municipal signage or other items commonly seen on the street. I wanted a simple base for the Tiran 5, an Israeli-modified T-55 in the Lebanese army, **12**.

I started, as before, with a palette-shaped base, **13**. (See, I told you I used this a lot!) But this time, I'm using one I cast from resin with sidewalks already in place.

After applying a white primer coat and letting it dry, I put down Tamiya thin masking tape where I wanted pavement markings, **14**. Some of the markings will be white and some will be yellow, **15**. I airbrushed the spaces I wanted yellow, let the paint dry, and then covered them with tape to protect them during the remaining painting steps.

With all the markings covered, I was ready to roll out (paint) some asphalt. The first coat was plain old Tamiya flat black. You want the first coat to cover, but you don't want it too thick, so a little streakiness is OK. It also makes the asphalt look more realistic.

camouflage and the markings on the German vehicle show that this unit was in Normandy. The scene I decided to model was a self-propelled gun pulled up next to a building and getting into position for an assault.

You can see some of the same elements as in the scene with the Luchs tank. In this vignette, I didn't have to scratch-build the parts, but instead cast duplicates in resin. (See chapter 6 for more on casting your own parts.) For example, the sidewalk is something I made and used copies of over and over again.

For the foundation, I started with a piece of plywood and covered it with Apoxie Sculpt (see photo on page 24). While the putty was still soft, I put very finely sifted, granulated dirt—real dirt—into the putty and pushed the vehicle into it to make tracks.

On top of the putty, I added a sidewalk, cobblestones, rubble, wall sections, and steps. The wall sections are resin-cast pieces of Custom Dioramics products, and I made the steps from Apoxie Sculpt. The cobblestone street is from VLS. By the steps is rubble from Custom Dioramics and VLS.

Notice that the street is not perpendicular to the vehicle. There's that rule of composition again: you don't want everything square, vertical, or horizontal. I angled the street and the sidewalk to offset the limitations of a square or rectangular design in attracting visual interest. Skewing it a little bit on the base looks more natural and not staged.

I also built up a little knoll to make the base visually more exciting, **11**. This definitely made the model building more interesting. I had to articulate the tank's

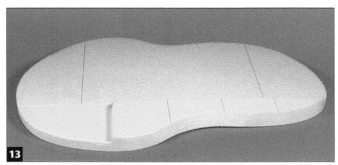

13

I cast this base from resin with the sidewalks already in place, which saved me a few steps while adding groundwork.

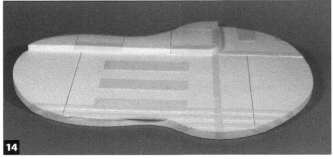

14

After the white primer dries, I use Tamiya tape to mask off lanes, crosswalks, and other markings at this intersection.

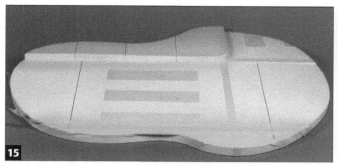

15 Some marks will be yellow. I airbrushed the yellow, waited for the paint to dry, then applied masking to keep those areas yellow.

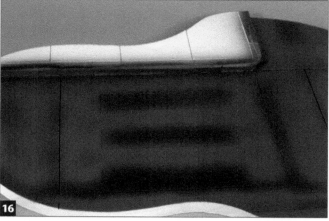

16 Airbrushed light gray and some blue (to represent oil streaks) built up over the flat-black base coat.

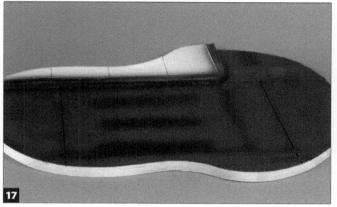

17 The different shades start to form familiar patterns in the pavement. The dark stripes are the tape strips covered by the first coat of black.

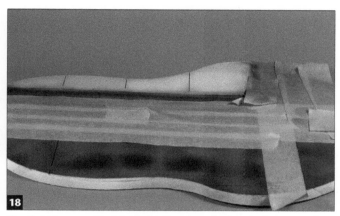

18 The light tan used to highlight the street is also the base coat for the sidewalk.

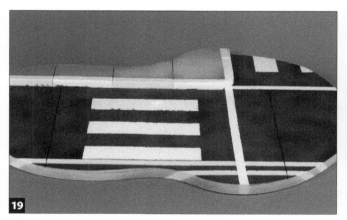

19 Off comes the tape, and the yellow and white traffic markings emerge.

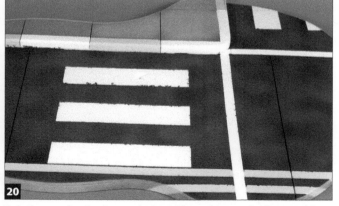

20 Painting perfection is not desired. The stripes and other markings look more realistic with little irregularities.

The next step was adding some different shades, **16**. I airbrushed highlights with lighter shades of gray and took a few swipes with a little blue to make the black asphalt look oily.

The overall effect of the lighter highlights was becoming apparent, **17**. I covered the areas that were good with some low-adhesive tape since I wasn't through highlighting. In fact, I mixed it up even more by adding some light tan highlights to make the asphalt look less uniform, **18**. The tan was also the first coat on the sidewalk.

Finishing the groundwork
When the paint dried, I lifted off all the tape to reveal the street surface and traffic markings, **19**. You'll notice that not all of the edges are perfect, and I didn't want

them to be, **20**. In Beirut, these markings are often painted by hand with a brush and are going to look a little ragged. Even the machines usually used in the States don't lay down perfectly clean edges. If cleaner edges are required for your locale, you can go back in and brush-paint them.

To finish the groundwork, I weathered the street with an artist's oil wash. A thin wash of burnt umber toned down the

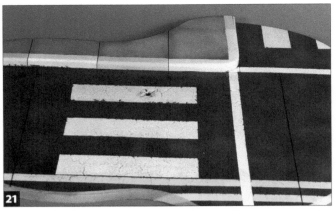

21 White and yellow paint doesn't stay clean too long on a street. A wash of burnt umber knocked the newness out of it.

22 A yellow ochre artist's oil wash (with just a tinge of jean brilliant mixed in) mutes the contrast of the burnt umber and provides highlights to edges.

23 After that, a wash of yellow ochre (lightened with flat white) unified the colors. Before it dried, I flowed a black wash into the recesses to make surface details jump out.

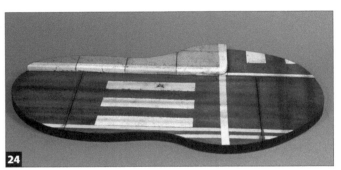

24 Airbrushing a repetition of the color layers—flat black, blue, light gray—produce the streaks you normally see in roadways.

25 At last, my street is open to heavy armor!

26

Using photos of Somalia, I came up with this base on which to show a scene of Mogadishu. The sandy groundwork includes rubble and tire tracks. I painted a faux wood finish on the base.

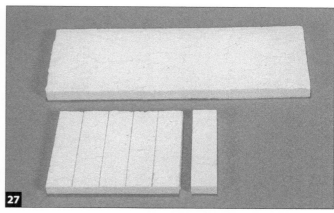

27

Simple resin castings can become part of a larger plan. Scribing lines make it easier to saw off smaller sections.

28

The structure is composed of various pieces cut from the basic slabs I cast in resin. I beveled some pieces (at left) to use on the base of the corner.

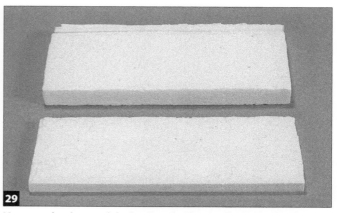

29

You can glue larger slabs back-to-back to make them thicker, as I have done here.

bright white paint, **21**. Then, over that went a wash of yellow ochre, **22**. I let that dry and then applied a wash of yellow ochre mixed with jean brilliant, a fleshy yellow color I really like. (You could use Naples yellow in its place.)

After that wash had dried, I repeated the yellow ochre wash, but lightened it with a little white, **23**. This really thin wash helped unify the colors and made the high spots visible.

While it was still wet, I followed with a black wash that flowed into all the cracks and textures to make surface details stand out. I also dipped a broad brush in the black wash and let most of the wash wick into a paper towel. I then pulled back the bristles and flicked tiny droplets of paint all over, spattering the base, to produce random spots of oil, other drippings, and stains. I repeated the spattering with a raw umber wash and then a yellow ochre one.

To add even more staining, and to blend the multicolored spatters, I returned with the airbrush and sprayed light streaks on the roadway to show exhaust and oil stains in the middle of a traffic lane, **24**. I started with black and then followed it using black with a little blue and gray mixed in to produce different shades and depths of color.

Finally, I painted the vertical edge of the base black—and then I was ready to open the street to my Lebanese Tiran 5, **25**.

Mogadishu in the 1990s

To develop this diorama of a Somalia technical (see chapter 10), I looked through a variety of photos of the country. I focused on finding buildings and other features that would give the scene a sense of place, **26**.

As I did, I came up with the idea of building a representative wall section out of cast-resin parts, **27**.

Being able to cast resin parts has many advantages. In addition to being able to make copies of almost anything you can build, you can design castings that can be used as building blocks, **28**. You can even glue like pieces together to double their thickness, **29**. I cut various pieces out of rectangular slabs to form the wall that became the backdrop of the scene.

The wall will be set on a simple base that I also cast from resin, **30**. Surrounding the wall will be sections of my homemade resin-cast sidewalk.

Behind the sidewalk, I built slots into the casting to accommodate the building. Since I was resin-casting the walls, too, I designed them with pour stubs that would fit the slots. That way, there was less cutting and sanding after I pulled the wall castings from their mold; I could just plug them in.

I textured the Apoxie Sculpt before it

30 The base features a big resin casting for my building section to stand on. You'll notice my sidewalk section (again). The blue flecks are from the RTV of the mold.

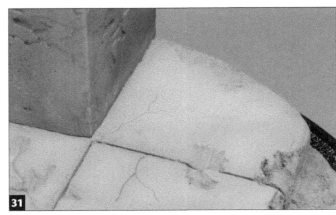

31 Brush-painting a wash brings out details. With the brush, I also added hairline cracks and other features.

32 More washes and powdered pigments provide color variation and, by adding darker tones in recesses, more depth. The swatch of paper with Arabic-looking characters doesn't actually say anything, but at this scale, it works.

33 A website provided the Coca-Cola sign image, à la Mogadishu, which I scaled to make a decal. After applying the decal, I painted some of the bullet holes and used filters and washes on it. Some of the weathering was done in Adobe Photoshop and was built into the image.

cured and used it for a master. That texture will stand out when painted.

I painted the sidewalk the base color, highlighted it with a lightened shade of the base color, and began applying washes, **31**. This painting process gave the sidewalk a little more depth and dimension.

Multiple layers of washes and pigments created a look of concrete poured over decrepit stonework, **32**. Near the sidewalk, I dropped in one of those little details that are important in providing the Wow Factor: a newspaper lies crumpled in the sand. I painted the letters to look like Arabic script, but there are no legible words. Being that small, from a distance it looks pretty doggone good!

After seeing a picture of a "Welcome to Mogadishu" billboard, I surfed the Internet some more and came up with a real Coca-Cola sign, **33**. I scaled it down to size in Adobe Photoshop, and also added some weathering with the software program. Weathering graphics on the computer is a touch that can help draw your eye to the scene and up the Wow Factor.

I then applied various filters and layers with oils and acrylics, and painted on the bullet holes.

To finish the base, I gave it a faux-wood paint job.

Desert Storm armor defilade

In the uncertain early stages of Operation Desert Storm, the media, in describing the Iraqi armor that would oppose the advance of the coalition forces, mentioned tanks in dug-out positions, or berms. Also called *defilades,* these emplacements were situated below the attackers' line of vision to defend against enemy fire.

While the defilades made for interesting explanatory graphics in television news reports, the tanks in those emplacements were no match for coalition armor. In fact, the tactic was to leave the Iraqi tanks right where they were and roll over the top of them.

I thought a defilade was yet another effective and unusual way to display an armor model, **34**.

Like the base I built for the Marder III, this one began with Styrofoam covered with Apoxie Sculpt. Then I added real dirt, which was coarser in this diorama to show a different texture than that shown in the Somali scene.

After preshading the deepest contours with Tamiya dark yellow (XF-60) darkened with flat black, I airbrushed the terrain with the dark yellow straight up, **35**. But the preshading remained in the corners and

34

Digging out a defilade—the berms described in reports during the early part of the First Gulf War—protected Iraqi tanks by keeping them below the line of fire. However, it couldn't keep coalition tanks from driving over them.

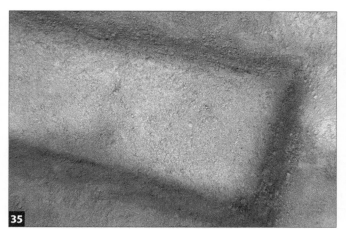

35

Deep in the corners, I airbrushed dark yellow darkened with flat black. I then oversprayed with dark yellow, which left the darker shade in place to define the shapes.

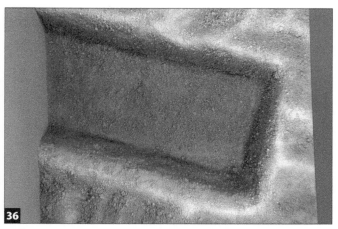

36

Airbrushing more dark yellow, lightened with flat white, hits the high spots. Following with mid-tones softens this effect.

recesses to define these features. Using an airbrush gave it soft edges, which is more conducive to graduating color.

Next, I mixed a little flat white with the dark yellow to exaggerate the highlights, **36**. Then I added some mid-tones to blend it together and lessen the contrast so it's not so dark and harsh.

In a close-up view, **37**, you can see the different layers of color that have been added, with the dark yellow base coat at the right, the darker preshade and washes in the corners, and the superhighlights in the upper left.

Next came some postshading, **38**. I introduced some more color variation in

the deepest spots using Tamiya khaki (XF-49). This left deeper shades in the recesses and lighter shades on the high spots.

Then, it was time for the artist's oils—and more mixing and blending. I first applied a wash of raw umber with a broad brush, **39**. I applied this pretty liberally,

37

What you might think of as a monochromatic terrain actually features several colors. From right to left is the dark yellow base coat, darker preshade and dark washes in the corner, and super-highlights on the ground at the top left.

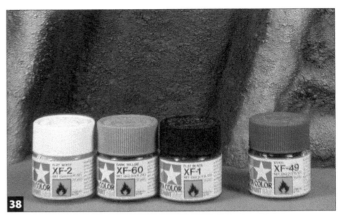

38

To deepen the recesses, I airbrushed them with Tamiya khaki. You can see the different browns and the deeper shades with black in the recesses, and the lighter shades on the high spots.

39

Truly painting with a broad brush: I applied an overall wash of raw umber to deepen the detail…

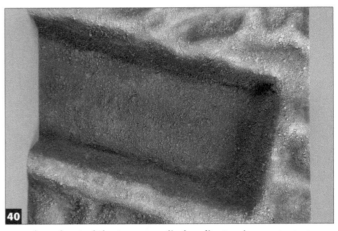

40

…and moderated the tones applied earlier to give a warmer overall appearance.

41

Dry-brushing with a mix of yellow ochre and a pinch of titanium white makes those pebbles pop.

42

When I completed the highlighting and test-fitting of the model, the defilade was ready for the T-55.

and it provided a darker, yet warmer overall look, **40**. The difference is subtle, but if you compare this photo to photo **36**, you can see how it changed.

Then, I applied more layers of various shades, now using raw umber mixed with varying amounts of Naples yellow. And to dry-brush highlights, I mixed a little yellow ochre with a touch of titanium white, **41**.

After completing one wash, I let it dry, and then went back and to see if I missed anything or needed to blend any areas better. Then I went on to the next wash. After each one, you can decide whether to tweak the color a little.

When I was satisfied, I test-fit the model, and the difilade was ready to be overrun by coalition forces, **42**.

43

I originally sculpted the master in Apoxie Sculpt and added footings for the pipeline, and then cast the whole thing in resin.

44

I built up the footings with bracketed pieces and Grandt Line bolts. The marks are for precise placement of the bolts.

45

Sections of clear acrylic rod form the pipeline. The markings are for more bolts to come.

46

The fittings are strip styrene and a big .040" styrene disc. The shutoff housing on top is a resin casting of mine.

Iranian desert pipeline patrol

Deserts come in all types, from the salt flats of Utah to the rock-and-tumbleweed barrens of the American Southwest. But what many of us think of first are the vast expanses of shifting sands seen through parts of North Africa and the Middle East.

That's the groundwork I needed for displaying the soldiers of the Pasdaran, who were riding the pipelines in the Iranian interior. (For more on the construction of this vignette, see chapter 11.)

From the ground up

On the base, I sculpted my "shifting sands" into dunes with Apoxie Sculpt, laying the putty down in the rough shape, then patterning the topography and adding rocks.

I have a half dozen or so different kinds of old, throwaway brushes I used to texture the surface (see Appendix). While the putty was still workable, I dipped a brush in water and stippled the putty, mixing it up with different brushes, to create my different terrain patterns.

Then I sprinkled a little bit of real fine dirt and silica sand over the surface and stippled it into place with the brushes, pushing it down into the putty to get a variety of textures. At that point, I positioned the jeep where I wanted it and made tracks in the putty, dirt, and sand

(but with another model so I didn't mess up the primary one).

I added footings for the pipeline supports, waited for everything to dry, and then cast the base in resin, **43**. The base was built similar to the one for the Mogadishu diorama, including a faux-wood finish on the pedestal.

The resin-casting is a step you can skip if you want—just proceed with an Apoxie Sculpt base. (I resin-cast the base so I can use one whenever I need one and not have to buy so much aftermarket stuff!)

I first worked on the pipeline footings. I added Grandt Line bolts and the bracketed pipeline stands, **44**.

47

With the pipelines in place, I checked the scene's composition. The second pipeline is ½" acrylic rod.

48

I angled the ends of the pipes, installed shutoff wheels, which came from spare parts, and then primed them.

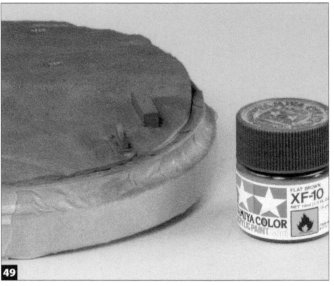

49

After masking the pedestal base, I primed the groundwork with Tamiya flat brown. Mixing a little dark yellow into the flat brown, I airbrushed a lighter coat that showed off the ups and downs of the terrain.

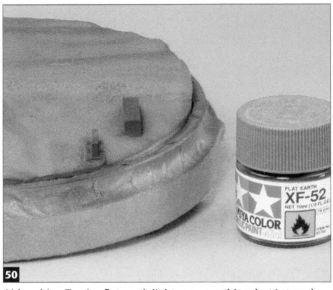

50

Airbrushing Tamiya flat earth lightens everything, but I stayed out of the deepest areas to keep them darker.

Next came the pipelines, **45**. I designed them using segments of solid clear acrylic rod that I got at a plastics store specializing in plastics for fabricating retail displays.

I added fittings made from strips and one .040" disc of styrene, and again, I marked them for precise bolt placement, **46**. The shutoff housing structure on the top was styrene I built up and cast in resin.

I placed the second pipe and tested the composition using the real jeep, not the junky one I used to make the tracks,

47. Then I primed everything (except the jeep, of course).

As this diorama took shape, I checked the composition so that the focal point remained dead center on the base. Your eyes should take you right to the hood of the jeep and the barrel of the recoilless rifle. See how the jeep sits a little farther back, because it overhangs a little? The barrel of the gun is centered with the centered mass of the pipeline.

I angled the ends of both rods at the edge of the base, like tangents to the circle beneath them, **48**. The shutoff wheels

are spare parts I pulled from a ¾-ton Dodge truck kit.

After pulling the pipes off, I masked the base's pedestal and primed the groundwork with flat brown (Tamiya XF-10), **49**.

For the next coat, I mixed the flat brown with Tamiya dark yellow (XF-60). I used this lighter shade to define contours.

To bring the terrain into greater relief, I airbrushed on a lighter, thin coat of Tamiya flat earth (XF-52), **50**. This hit the high spots, but I stayed away from the dark brown shadows.

I then airbrushed a dark yellow layer

51

A layer of dark yellow provides more color variation. It ties into the earlier, darker mix that contains some dark yellow, so this coat provides both detail and unity.

52

Highlighting coats of lightened dark yellow bring the high spots into relief.

53

An umber wash settles in the low spots while dry-brushing provides additional highlights.

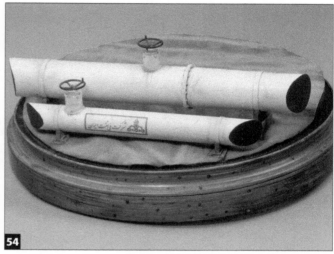

54

Adding a decal for the oil company, weathering around the fittings with some umber washes, and paining the pipe ends black completed the pipelines.

over the flat earth for even more variation, **51**. This also unified it with the underlying coats, which contained some dark yellow.

Then I added some superhighlights by mixing a little white to the dark yellow and turning up the contrast with the shadowy recesses, **52**. I then airbrushed a darkened

shade of flat earth into those recesses, turning up the contrast again but at the same time homogenizing the shades.

An umber wash and some final dry-brushing with lighter shades completed the terrain. Then I was ready to install the pipes, **53**.

I painted the angled pipe ends flat black to reinforce the illusion that they continued to some distant refinery depot, **54**. I added a custom-made decal to the smaller pipe that I designed from images I found in my research. The base was then ready for the inspection patrol.

REFERENCES

Here are some valuable books in preparing groundwork and scenery elements.

Then and Now series (After the Battle): These books provide a look at past battles and recent photos of the site for comparison. I consider those books gospel.

Manhole Covers, Mimi and Robert Melnick (MIT Press): Now *this* is specialized, although you'll notice that a manhole cover plays a prominent part in the scene on this book's cover.

The Elements of Style: A Practical Encyclopedia of Interior Architectural Details from 1485 to the Present, Stephen Calloway and Elizabeth Cromley (Simon & Schuster): The title says it all.

Surfaces: Visual Research for Artists, Architects, and Designers, Judy Juracek (W. W. Norton): It includes more than 1,200 photos of different surface textures.

3

Wonderful wedgies

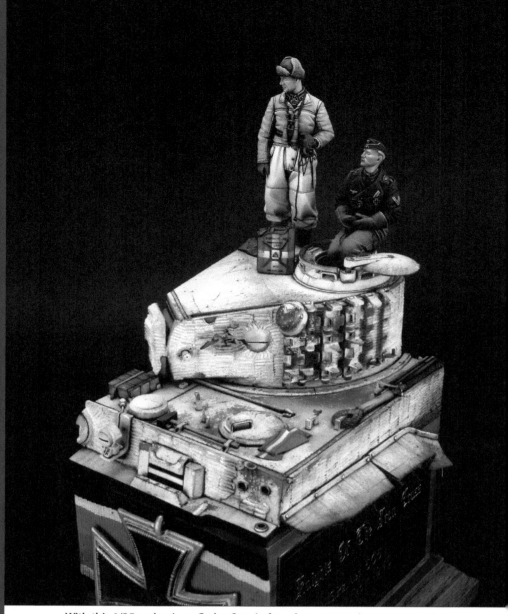

With this 1/35 scale piece, Carlos Startin found a very creative way to maximize what a wedgie can do. Concentrating on the two figures, he didn't have to do groundwork, show tracks in mud, or even build tank tracks to help tell the story. Plus, he found a way to make a two-sided display of the base. *Marcus Nicholls, courtesy of Tamiya Model Magazine International*

A wedgie is what I call a partial model sliced off almost as you would crop a picture, **1**. Wedgies can be dramatic attention-getters, but it takes advanced modeling skills to make them look well executed, rather than something crudely sawed off, **2**. You could call them part of a vignette or a cut-down diorama. With what you might do to the model, it could literally be a "slice of life." When I developed this concept, I was thinking of a slice of pie—a wedge.

1 Finns fight the Soviets in World War II: this is a Warriors Scale Model figure I converted years ago. Cropped like a photo, this wedgie implies space and provides context without even a vehicle. As on most wedgies, the abrupt terminus is painted flat black to make it clear that it's an edge.

2 This 1/35 scale piece by Carlos Startin utilizes a prebuilt wedgie from Darius Miniatures of Poland. The sectioned vehicle is a late-war Hetzer. Carlos gave it a hairspray-release weathering treatment to distress the winter camouflage. Color modulation mimics light, with the lighter shades at the top and lower surfaces and recesses darkened. The snow is sandblasting grit mixed with white glue, and more glue shows melting snow. Carlos converted an Alpine figure and gave it a dejected-looking head from Hornet. He used artist's oils throughout, with shading based on zenithal lighting principles. *Marcus Nicholls, courtesy of Tamiya Model Magazine International*

Marcus Nicholls, courtesy of Tamiya Model Magazine International

3 On this premade wedgie from Darius Miniatures of Poland, Carlos Startin models a section of a Tiger I tank and a figure in a way that draws viewers to the wedgie. The surrounding equipment (from LionRoar) makes a statement about fuel shortages for the Panzer Korps late in the war.

4 Robert Döpp goes big with this 1/16 scale project. This mostly scratchbuilt wedgie is packed with more added detail than you usually find on an entire vehicle. The cutaway reveals the interior of a Panther turret; dark gray pieces on the outside are resin castings Robert made by modifying Tamiya kit pieces. Other than a few photoetched-metal pieces from Aber, it's all Robert—he sculpted the two figures. This portrait of two tankers having a smoke and scanning the sky for aircraft is called "Lucky Guys." *Robert Döpp*

Although only the front half is shown, you can easily imagine this T-34 in its entirety. For my money, the versatile T-34 tanks make the best wedgies. Almost every facet of this famous vehicle is easy to identify. Plus, there's a wide chronological window to work with. You can show these tanks in early, mid, or late postwar in Russia, Berlin, or even the Middle East.

Carlos Startin built a 1/35 scale prefabricated wedgie made by a Polish company, Blackdog, added bits of kits from Dragon, and put a Hornet head on an Alpine Miniatures figure that he painted with oils. The SdKfz 251 Ausf C is readily identifiable just from its hindquarters. From the clothing and camouflage, we also know it's on the Eastern Front. *Marcus Nicholls, courtesy of Tamiya Model Magazine International*

One reason I created this format was that it's a lot of work doing a whole diorama. You build a vehicle, put figures with it, and do all the groundwork. Then when you display it, it often doesn't get the attention it deserves as people will glance at it and walk past it. So I created the wedgie to make people stop and look. Having just a section of a vehicle with a figure creates excitement and curiosity, and people are more inclined to stop and look at your piece, **3**. You can still put a lot of work into a wedgie, but you can superdetail a tank and not spend a lifetime doing it, **4**. I don't want to say it's a quick and dirty process of creating a miniature diorama, but it definitely expedites the process and you can actually put more into it.

In a well-constructed wedgie, you can produce the same story or aesthetic results by only doing a portion of a model because subconsciously a viewer sees the whole model, even though there's just a piece of it there, **5**.

One of the tricks of doing a wedgie is knowing the essential portion of what you want to show. Whether it's a vehicle, building, or an airplane, if you're going to cut

it, you need to pick the one section that best makes it identifiable, **6**. You need to know the minimum portion of what you can show—or the maximum of what you can do without (or get away with), **7**. Especially if you're working with a small part of a model, you have to use the one salient feature that is identifiable by itself, **8**.

It's about the figure

The wedgie is a format that honors the figure. Whereas figures are often placed in a diorama to give an aircraft or vehicle scale, in a wedgie, it's the other way around—you want part of a model to give emphasis to the figure. It's a tighter focus that ensures what you are trying to show with the figure doesn't get lost in a lot of other details, **9**.

What goes with the figure must be essential. For example, you could take a distinctive vehicle, such as a Panther, Sherman, or T-34 tank, and cut a section of the tank that shows the drive sprocket, a recognizable portion of the hull, or part of the front of the turret, **10**.

The figure's pose, its uniform, or the time period of the setting are factors to

consider when composing a wedgie, **11**. You have to play around with different ideas, including objects to pose with a figure. Also, imagine what you want the character doing. If the scene is set in the desert, you could have him stand in front of the tank and crack an egg onto the glacis plate, watching the egg cook on the front of the tank. (There are actual photos of this.)

Posing figures in front of an airplane can be problematic. You may see a picture of several airmen in front of a bomber, but it's hard to get the same perspective when building a full model on a display base. If you have several 1/72 scale figures standing in front of a B-17, you don't really see much going on. But for a more effective scene, you could make a wedgie that shows a pilot getting out of a fighter plane's cockpit by just using the nose section or another part of the plane, **12**.

A wedgie makes efficient use of space. It is a way to imply something much greater in size. You may pose a figure amongst the rubble of a street battle or in a more natural setting. But you need to go

7

In this wedgie by Harold "Hap" Wolfgram, Wehrmacht soldiers surrender to Canadian soldiers. There's more vehicle than I would use here, but it fills out Hap's composition. This simplified vignette definitely presents a clear message.

8

A 1/35 scale wedgie by Greg Cihlar not only demonstrates a minimal representation of the vehicle but also the compositional rule of thirds, both laterally and vertically.

9

This is one of my earliest wedgies—in fact, the first one that turned out well. Half-tracks are harder to do because you need to show some vehicle interior. I dodged around a little by showing this part of the vehicle; otherwise, I might have had to show additional details, which would have been a distraction and taken focus away from the figure.

beyond the bricks or grass. The model and figures tell the story, **13**.

Practical considerations

The one thing I hate doing is just taking a stock figure and placing it on a wooden base with a label on the front. I want to be able to bring that figure to life. If I enter something in a competition, every little

bit of creativity I can display gives me an advantage. It's that little kick you need to get someone to stop and take a look at your model.

But it can be risky. Before cutting up a new model, are you willing to sacrifice part of a model for the sake of the figure? I have had a few attempts at wedgie building that just didn't work, and I had to scrap them. I

have three or four models sitting here right now that are pretty messed up. I'm not immune to massive screw-ups!

It takes a little courage to cut up a model to construct a wedgie. But you can also look and see if you have some spare model parts lying around that might work instead of sacrificing an entire model. I've also taken a tank and cut it in two, and

10 In East Prussia, 1945, a German grenadier places a mine on the tracks of a Soviet T-34/85. For this wedgie, I took an old 1/35 scale Tamiya model of a T-34, sawed it off, and posed its easily identifiable front section. The bricks are hand-laid over a hollow base for the effect of the open manhole.

11 Based on 1/35 scale Think 180 Studios figures, Artur Miniszewski's "Streets of Baghdad" is an excellent example of minimalism, with fragments of highly recognizable objects surrounding the detailed figures. People familiar with Baghdad streets will recognize the roll-down garage door, and everybody knows a Volkswagen bug when they see it.

12 John Rosengrant's pilot figure doesn't need much around it—just the cockpit section of a P-51, which is easy to recognize. While this portion of aircraft is faithfully reproduced, the emphasis is clearly on the figure. And that is the purpose of a wedgie, a format that honors the figure. George Preddy was the top P-51 ace of World War II. *John Rosengrant*

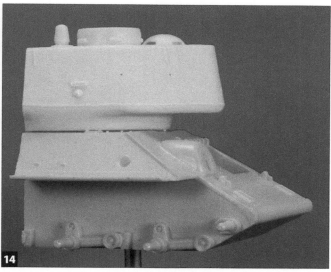

13 This 1/9 scale wedgie cuts both vehicle and figure to the essential. The American tanker is actually a self-portrait by John Rosengrant. This is a production version of a piece to which he later added a complete turret, put a letter in the tanker's hand, and called it "Dear John."

14 Cutting a model in half may be a little scary, but after sawing a T-34 in two, I was able to use this front section for one wedgie and the back portion for another.

15 In a wedgie I call "Stalin's Taxi," set in Berlin, 1945, the soldiers demonstrate a common Soviet infantry tactic of riding into battle by hitching a ride on the deck of a T-34. Each side of the wedgie offers a different view of the action taken by the soldiers.

built one wedgie out of the front and another out of the back, **14**.

Additionally, now that the model industry has advanced through several generations of new toolings, and with today's technology making model manufacturing better than ever, it doesn't make sense to cut up a new, more expensive kit to use for a wedgie. Quality, older models work well and will spare your modern, high-tech kits. And, of course, if you have a model that got botched or broken, sections of it could find new life in a wedgie.

Imagine the plan

I've seen some wedgies that just didn't work. As you plan the project, it's important to visualize the story you want to tell and how the figure and other models work together to tell it. A wedgie showing a figure standing with his hand on the wingtip of an airplane doesn't tell you much. But a wedgie with an American figure standing next to the shot-up rudder of a Bf 109G, which has a very distinctive cut, can be more effective. That's minimal but clear, and it's more creative

than just having the figure standing alone on a base.

When building a wedgie, don't feel that you're limited to one figure or one model, **15**. You're constrained only by your thoughts and your creativity. Think of it as a snapshot picture. In the wedgie format, you're abbreviating the model to more clearly tell a story. So, it's critical to have a clear idea of what's going to be in that picture before you begin. And, when you're through, if you've done a fair job of it, viewers will have a clear picture too.

4

Figure painting

Accompanying Cambodian Khmer Krom mercenaries, Special Forces SPEC4 Fletcher Clement (right) wears tiger-striped fatigues and a very rare military hat. Called a brimmed jungle hat, it was issued only in 1964 in olive drab (OD 107). It never caught on as Special Forces preferred the beret. *Fletcher Clement*

Here's another look at Fletcher in that uniform. These were notoriously ill-fitting fatigues; the trousers and sleeves were never long enough for Americans. *Fletcher Clement*

The purpose of a diorama is to put your models in a lifelike setting. And nothing does that as well as human figures. You may not be familiar with an aircraft or an armored vehicle, but seeing a human figure posed with it immediately expresses the scale of whatever you build. A human figure provides a measurement we all know.

Yet many modelers are not confident in their ability to paint figures, especially faces. That's because they know that nothing can ruin a display more quickly than a flawed or poorly painted figure. It's a mistake everyone can see.

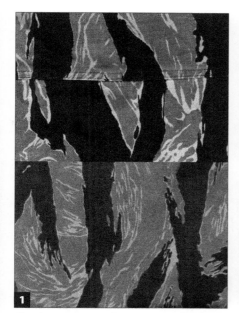

1

The tiger-stripe uniforms varied quite a bit, even in a single uniform. Here, the upper portion is from the trousers; the lower part is the shirt from the same uniform, but it is much more faded looking.

2

I kept this worksheet on my workbench throughout the project. In addition to the paint samples and notes on the right, I included five images, including two close to 1/16 scale, of the uniform.

3

To prep the figure, I sprayed it with Brite Touch automotive primer. The primer provided a firm footing for the acrylic base colors that follow.

Excellence in scale figure modeling is the realm of master painters familiar with the human form. However, you don't have to be a Rembrandt to make your figures look effective. I'm going to share specific figure painting techniques that can add life to inanimate sculptures and allow them to support and enhance your dioramas—or to even stand alone as a piece of art in its own right.

Camouflage

I've done extensive research on tiger stripe uniforms, and believe me, there are a lot of variations. I generally go by the book *Tiger Patterns: A Guide to the Vietnam War's Tigerstripe Combat Fatigue Patterns and Uniforms* by Sgt. Richard Denis Johnson (Shiffer).

One of the biggest problems with maintaining accuracy is the variety from the manufacturers. If the uniforms were made in Vietnam, there was no standardization of patterns or fit. In the photo of Fletcher on the opposite page, you can see how much the uniforms vary.

Even a single uniform weathers differently. A shirt can fade differently from the trousers. Maybe it got more sun, or maybe the fabric was printed at a different time.

As an example, photo **1** shows swatches from one uniform. The lower one, from the shirt, looks muted and dull. Above it are the trousers, which look sharper and newer.

As I worked on this project, I created a worksheet that kept my references at hand. It contained five images, notes, and my palette, **2**. The larger image at top is a section of the actual uniform, which I scanned in. I added two photos showing the front and back of the uniform.

To get a sense of scale, as I was hand-painting the pattern, I reduced the front and back shots close to 1/16 scale and placed them above my palette. My palette contained mostly Lifecolor paint numbers. I dabbed a little paint there and tried different colors for a match.

I printed all the photos on glossy photo paper so I could review the colors. (But the colors in the front and back shots look nothing like those of the scanned uniform above it.)

This was my general setup to keep track of what I was doing as I progressed through the project. It was great if I had to go back and touch something up, paint outlines, or mix shades for highlights and shadows. That way, I was able to remember what I used.

TIP: I put a couple of dabs on the paint cap to make it easier to see the colors as I worked.

I started the bust by spraying on a coat of Brite Touch automotive lacquer primer, **3**. It covers great and dries fast! I wanted to make sure the acrylics would adhere. Acrylics want to slide around on resin, so it can take three or four coats before they grab. The primer puts different paints on an even footing.

TIP: This is a good time to look for any flaws in the figure and smooth them out.

For the base color, I selected olive drab M1943 (Lifecolor UA421). (With so many colors in play, I took no chances and wrote the base-coat color right on the base.)

Next, I chose a tan color for the tiger stripes in the camo pattern, **4**. I mixed 50:50 Reaper Terran khaki and Lifecolor olive drab yellow tone. Popular with those who like to paint game figures, Reaper paint is available in game shops. When you apply it with a brush, the paint levels out and the brush strokes disappear.

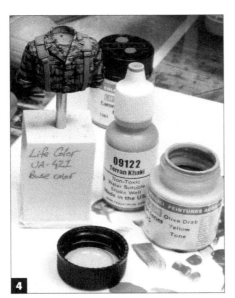

4

The lighter color in the camo pattern is a 1:1 mix of Lifecolor olive drab yellow tone and Reaper Terran khaki.

5

After the primer coat, I brush-painted the olive drab base coat, as I would all the succeeding paint layers.

6

I highlighted the raised areas by painting them a mix of 7 parts base color to 3 parts flesh, with a dab of white to lighten it a bit more.

Underneath the pattern

I brush-painted the base coat, **5**. I didn't have to thin the Lifecolor paint very much. You could airbrush it, but I usually brush-paint figures. When using an airbrush, you might get some spitting paint or atomization that can make the surface look powdery. (I might use an airbrush on a bigger figure, like 1/9 scale, but 1/16 is a lot smaller than it looks. This bust is only 1.5" wide and 2" tall with the head on it.) The base might take two or three coats to cover.

Next came the shadows. I added Reaper black (but it could be any black) to the Lifecolor base coat. The mix was about a 7:3 mix of the base to black.

I followed the shadows with highlights, **6**. For this step, I used the base color plus some flesh (about a 7:3 mix) and lightened with a little white.

I added the shadows and highlights before painting the camouflage, so they would show through. Trying to highlight

MY INSPIRATION

I usually sculpt and paint 1/35 scale figures. But to demonstrate these techniques, I chose something about twice as big—a 1/16 scale bust of a Vietnam-era Special Forces officer by Miniatures PMC: 1st Lt. 5th S.F. (CDIG/Mike Force), Republic of Vietnam, 1963-66 (No. PMC-16001).

At an annual gathering of the Military Miniatures Society of Illinois, I was discussing a camouflage pattern I had painted with a fellow who turned out to be Fletcher Clement, a world-renowned figure sculptor and painter.

"You certainly seem to know a lot about camouflage," I said. "Well, yeah," he said. Fletcher served with Special Forces in Vietnam in 1965 and '66. I asked him if he had any pictures, and he drawled, "Yeah, I've got a few." Then he pulled one out of his billfold, and I knew he wasn't kidding!

About a month later, on a trip to Dallas, I decided to pay Fletcher a visit in Little Rock. I scanned all his photos for him, put them on his computer, and burned discs. We had a nice time, went out for dinner, and the next day I went on to Dallas.

A couple of months went by, and two weeks before Christmas a package showed up in the mail. It was from Fletcher: one of his uniforms—one he wore—the real deal. And it was a uniform that's hard to come by: official-issue "John Wayne Dense Pattern" (JWD) tiger-striped combat fatigues. The beret and the hat were a loan, he said, but I could keep the rest. I was blown away.

The tiger stripes are one of the most famous American patterns, and one of the harder ones to paint. I've painted them in 1/35 scale before, but never in 1/16 scale. You can get by with some things in 1/35 scale that you can't in 1/16. When it's bigger, you have to show your work, so it's got to be dead-on.

But now I had the perfect reference sitting right there next to me. I also had three pictures of Fletcher in that uniform. Although I knew I couldn't paint on resin in 1/16 scale as well as you can print on fabric, I thought I could be pretty exact.

Then rather than model a generic soldier, I decided to portray a real person—and a real hero: Special Forces 1st Lt. George "Kenny" Sisler, of Dexter, Mo. (Dexter is a small town in the Missouri boot heel, close to Arkansas.) He was a classmate of my father-in-law, who remembered Kenny as a fun-loving class clown, always in a little trouble here and there. On his second tour in Vietnam in 1967, Kenny gave his life for his country. For his valor in combat, he was awarded the Medal of Honor.

I had plenty of inspiration to get me going on this project: the sacrifice Kenny made, the stories my father-in-law told me about him, Fletcher's uniform, and the tales he told.

7

Camouflage will later cover the sharp contrast between shadows and highlights, but they will still show through.

8

The camo pattern begins with a faded black; I added a little flesh and blue to the black to give it that faded appearance. If you look at the lapels, you can see the highlights under the camouflage.

9

I outlined the black tiger stripes with the second camo color to complete the pattern. You can see how the direction of pattern varies on different sections of the shirt.

and shadow over the camouflage doesn't work well, and, if you do, it could take forever.

At this stage, the contrast of highlights and shadows appeared very stark, **7**. Later, a lot of this would be covered with camouflage, yet the effects would still show through.

TIP: The best way to judge where to emphasize shadows and highlights is to place a figure right under a single lamp (turn off all the other lights in the room). This gives you a look at the most prominent highlights and deepest shadows. Sometimes I'll take a photo of the figure and keep it by my workbench as reference.

The first layer of the camouflage pattern was black, lightened with a little flesh and a little blue to show fading, **8**. The black doesn't have to be pretty, but it should have sharp edges. It's a disruptive pattern calculated to hide or "disrupt" the true shape of the body inside the uniform.

A lot of modelers make the mistake of painting the whole uniform as a one-unit piece. They paint over the pockets without thinking about the fabric and how it was sewn together. On real uniforms, the patterns on the pockets might not run in the same direction as the pattern on the shirt

or pants because the pockets were sewn onto them. Around seams, such as those on shirt sleeves, the patterns change. The patterns aren't even the same coming across the horizontal. It depends on how the fabric was cut. In the back, the pattern on the collar runs vertically—perpendicular to the shirt, **9**.

I used the second color (50:50 Reaper Terran khaki and Lifecolor olive drab yellow tone) to outline the black pattern. Again, this second camouflage color can vary depending on factors such as the light source its seen in, the printing of the fabric, the printing of a photograph, or the fading of the fabric. It can look like anything from a pale green to something near yellow. What I matched up came out pretty close to khaki. Since the webbing goes over the shirt, you have to connect the pattern on both sides of the webbing, **10**.

Uniform details

After working on the camo pattern, I turned my attention to some of the uniform details. I painted the webbing a darker shade of green—webbing can be hundreds of different shades of greens and khakis, **11**.

The buttons were base-coated with the same color as the webbing, but I dropped in shadows and highlights to make them look more three-dimensional.

To outline the stitching on the sleeves and collar, I used the highlight colors.

I researched the markings from photo sources and hand-painted them. The Special Forces patch on the bicep is Reaper marine teal (No. 09077), **12**. I outlined the patch by adding a little bit of white to the teal. I painted the sword and lightning bolts with yellow artist's acrylics: a golden yellow base, and then a flat yellow with just a drop of white over that to highlight.

The Airborne tag took me five tries to get right! I first tried to paint it with oils. That looked OK at first, but the yellow oil kept seeping into the black and wouldn't dry. So I scraped it all that off and started over with acrylics.

I painted Sisler's name tag and other patches to look as if they lie beneath the webbing, **13**. The American lieutenant's bar is on the collar, and the equivalent South Vietnamese rank is signified by the two stars on the chest. The shield on the breast pocket is a Mike Force patch.

With the uniform completely painted, you can still see the effects of shadow and highlights, especially on the stitching and the webbing, under the camouflage, **14**. It's all from the same sequence of painting—base, shadow, highlights, and outlining superhighlights.

Now it was time to put a face with that uniform.

10

As I continued to outline, I left the pattern off the uniform patches. I also painted around the webbing, continuing the pattern as if it were passing underneath the belts.

11

Now we're getting somewhere. All the patches and lettering were hand-painted. The webbing was painted a darker shade of olive drab, shaded and highlighted to distinguish the details.

12

It might have been made for painting game figures, but Reaper marine teal was the perfect color for the Special Forces patch on the bicep.

Painting faces

I used two colors of Vallejo acrylics for a flesh-tone base: a 1:1 mix of dark flesh and orange brown, **15**. It usually takes two or three thin coats to cover. I brushed on a coat, dried it quickly with a blow-dryer, and then painted it again.

Next, I went right over it with artist's oils to shade the flesh. I used five colors of artist's oils on the face, **16**. Additionally, I used crimson, red, rose, or burgundy to base-coat the lips.

I use oils because I have not perfected the art of painting faces with acrylics. With acrylics, you don't blend so much as you layer paint. If you look at a face painted with acrylics, you see sharper, harsher contrasts between light and shadow.

On the other hand, you can smear oils around more. They take longer to dry, so you can go back and forth as many times as you need to adjust color or shade. With oils, once you have the look you want, you can take a large No. 6 Filbert brush, with its rounded tip, and gently draw it across the face to pull highlights or shadows with it. (You can get a look at a No. 6 Filbert and the other brushes I use in the Appendix.) Or if you are still adjusting, you can blend highlights and shadow together and redefine them.

Base coat

After priming and base-coating the head with that 1:1 mix of dark flesh and orange brown, **17**, I added a wash of burnt umber artist's oil, **18**. (It doesn't look pretty at this stage, but it'll get better.) Apply the wash with a flat brush and let it sit for a minute or two, but don't let it dry! Then take a dry, flat brush and remove all the excess. Next, take a soft, lint-free cloth—an old T-shirt works, but don't use a paper towel—and drag the wash off the brush. I repeated this process until the face had an even, thin coat of burnt umber with darkened recesses.

Highlights and blending

Over this layer goes an aggressive application of highlights, **19**. (And those are big highlights!) I started this step immediately after removing the excess burnt umber wash—you don't want it to dry. I put pure titanium white where I wanted the highlights.

This is another time to look at a figure under a single, direct light and determine where the biggest highlights need to go. You can adjust the highlights or even take them off and do it again. Oils' slow drying time will let you do that.

After the bright dabs were applied, I began the blending process, **20**. This is the

first stage of blending highlights, or what I call the *base-color highlights*. I used a small Filbert brush to blend the white into the burnt umber wash underneath. Don't be timid with it, just brush it around and into the background or base color.

TIP: Make sure your brushes are clean. If they're just sitting out on your desk, they're getting dusty. Then when you start painting, you'll see little shreds of fuzz showing up in your paint. I always clean my brushes thoroughly with lacquer thinner and let them dry before I paint.

This was just the first step. Go over it, clean it up, blend it in, feather the highlights out, and add contrast and tone as you blend it. You'll see how the nose, the forehead, the cheekbones, the muscle in the neck, and the ears start to take on life.

Shadowy washes and more blending

Once the highlights are blended, you need to further define the shadows, **21**. I painted a 1:1 mix of burnt sienna and burnt umber into the places where deep shadows should be: crevices, recesses, under the lip of the beret, under the eyebrows, under the lips, and on each side of the nose. The dash of color across the

13 In this view, you can see how that sharply contrasted undercoating has softened to subtly emphasize billows and folds in the fabric. The contrast is less obvious but still visible.

14 You have to work carefully around the webbing to paint the patches and tags so it looks as if they are partially covered by the belts. There's a lieutenant's bar on the collar, and the equivalent South Vietnamese rank is on the chest.

15 These were the two colors I used for base-coating the flesh: Vallejo dark flesh and orange brown.

cheek will become a bit of a shadow when it's blended; same for the sides of the nose, under the jaw, and inside the ear.

I used a small Filbert brush to blend the shadows. A stippling motion, up and down, pushed that layer around and into folds and wrinkles on the face. Where the colors border, dab them together, merge their edges, and feather them. Once those colors are blended, take a larger Filbert brush and lightly stroke in one direction—front to back or top to bottom—and drag off the excess. Finally, enough is enough. The more artist's oils on the face, the more likely this paint is going to slide around and not adhere.

The face was roughed out now. It will take two or three days for oils to dry. As they dry, you can still go back and add highlights and shadows to get more definition.

You can get the paint to dry faster. Set the bust in a gas stove, with just the pilot light on, and it will dry overnight. You can even get it to dry faster. I set the bust on a block of wood inside a cheap little crock pot, and it will dry in an hour. (Note: This is for resin—don't try it with styrene!)

Adding more details

After the oils dried, I was ready to add more details to the face. I used cadmium red with a little white for a rose color on the neck, cheeks, earlobes, and edges of the nostrils, **22**. Blending those colors in gave the complexion a rosy look, **23**.

After that wash and blending, I went deeper, precisely brushing in darker details, **24**. I used burnt umber to outline deeper shadows, putting paint on the temple, the lip of the beret, the bridge of the nose, the creases in the cheeks, and the ridges under the nose as well as under the brow and under the lips. On the right side of the face, I used less burnt umber to show that this side is in the sun. I used paint to suggest lighting.

16 I used at lease five colors of artist's oils to help shade and detail the face.

17 Here's the base coat: a 1:1 mix of dark flesh and orange brown. Two or three light coats of this mix will do.

18 It looks awful now, but the burnt umber wash will settle into low spots and bring raised details into greater relief. Brushing and blending will take away the ugliness.

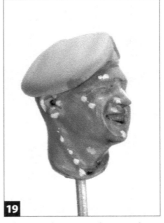

19 After the burnt umber wash, I added stark highlights of pure titanium white. There will be a lot of blending, but this certainly livens things up and brings high spots into even greater relief.

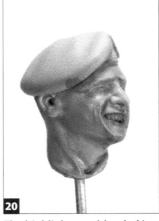

20 The highlights are blended in, which leaves the face with an aura of illumination.

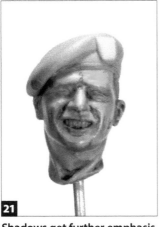

21 Shadows get further emphasis by brushing a 1:1 mix of burnt sienna and burnt umber into the deepest recesses and hollows.

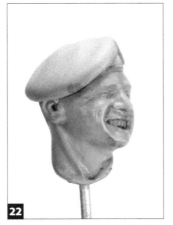

22 After the previous oils dried, I took a more detailed approach to selectively calling out features. I applied cadmium red, lightened with a little white, to the lips and the rosier features of the face, including a little color for ruddy cheeks.

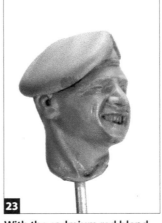

23 With the cadmium red blended, this guy is beginning to look like he's been in the sun.

24 I used bold strokes of burnt umber to define creases, folds, wrinkles, and shadowed parts of the face. On the left side, I used less burnt umber. This side is in the sun, and I used paint to suggest light.

As I feathered the burnt umber from these deep spots to blend them, the face became further defined, **25**. Now you could see the rosy colors and the deep shadows. You can let this layer dry, and come back and put oils over it. Although it won't blend in, because the oils under it have dried, you can overpaint it. If you want, you can blend in additional colors using a small, stubby brush with just a little thinner on so it's barely damp.

TIP: Remember that a little oil goes a long way. When you start blending, it can really spread out into a big area. So, easy does it. You can always add a little more if needed.

Adding more highlights
As I neared the end of the painting process, I added another coat of highlights to brighten and refresh the colors. As before, they were bold strokes of titanium white, but even more selectively applied, **26**.

There was less blending here. I directed these highlights to the brightest spots: teeth, cheek, chin, and eyebrows—those parts of the face that catch the most light.

There is not as much highlighting on the sides now. The definition is already present, and you want the front part of the face to pop out, so the highlighting on the sides is very sparse, just tiny dabs. A little blending gave the face a look of illumination, **27**. After this step, I baked

25 Brushing and blending produces a face with even more detail and definition of light. You still see the shadows in deep folds and under the brow and jaw.

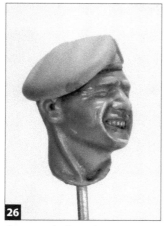

26 Once again, I used pure titanium white for highlights, but this time, I used them much more selectively, aimed specifically at the most prominent features.

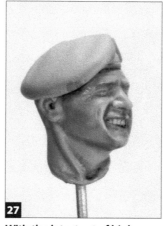

27 With the latest set of highlights blended, I was able to get the high contrast of bright lighting seen in many photos of Vietnam. Then, I let everything dry again before proceeding.

28 Here, I painted the eye sockets black and flowed burnt umber into the mouth to deepen and detail it.

29 The "whites" of the eyes are actually the same base color as the skin (1:1 mix of Vallejo dark flesh and orange brown). I left the iris and the very edges of the eyes black for the moment.

30 The hair is burnt umber acrylic lightened with a little flesh. I faded it at the top and front and blended it back with a lighter shade. Then I stroked in a little burnt umber for detail and lessened the contrast with a light coat of highlights.

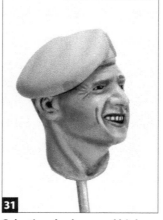

31 Selective shadows and highlights bring out features like the crow's feet around the eyes and the dimpled cheeks.

32 I painted the irises Reaper marine teal. A tiny highlight in the lower quadrant of each iris brings the eyes to life.

the face in the crockpot for 90 minutes, so I could overpaint details without smearing the underlying paint.

Adding final details

The final steps in painting the bust include doing the hair, lips, and eyes.

I first painted the eye sockets with Vallejo flat black acrylic. I thinned the black but not too much. You want to be able to get the paint in there, but you don't want it running all over, **28**.

Also at this time, I painted details in the mouth with Golden burnt umber artist's acrylic.

Returning to the eyes, we go from black to white. The "whites" of the eyes are not really white. I painted them with the skin's base color (1:1 mix of Vallejo dark flesh and orange brown). I worked around the perimeter of the iris and left a thin black lining around the edges of the eyes, **29**.

In photo **29**, you can see the eyebrow on the right being painted. I started with the

base skin color and then added a little black to darken the eyebrow. I returned with the base color, painting inside the edges of the eyebrow. I even stroked some hair into the eyebrow. At the top of the eye socket, under the brow, I added a bit of shadow using a maroon/brown shade.

TIP: It's important to have the proper amount of paint. Check the viscosity before you start. Load the brush and twist it on the base of your thumb to see how thick it is.

33

Here, the same pattern of selective shadowing and highlights further distinguishes the hair and the shape of the beret. You also see contrasts that define features on the cheek, ear, and neck.

34

And here he is: 1st Lt. George K. Sisler, a war hero who made the ultimate sacrifice fighting for his country.

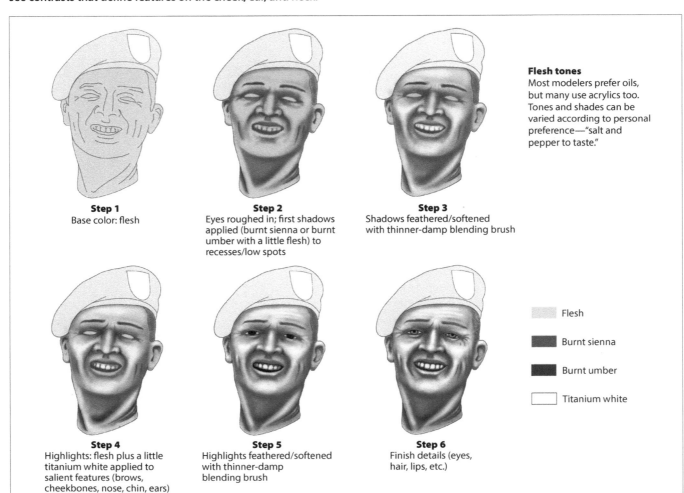

Step 1
Base color: flesh

Step 2
Eyes roughed in; first shadows applied (burnt sienna or burnt umber with a little flesh) to recesses/low spots

Step 3
Shadows feathered/softened with thinner-damp blending brush

Step 4
Highlights: flesh plus a little titanium white applied to salient features (brows, cheekbones, nose, chin, ears)

Step 5
Highlights feathered/softened with thinner-damp blending brush

Step 6
Finish details (eyes, hair, lips, etc.)

Flesh tones
Most modelers prefer oils, but many use acrylics too. Tones and shades can be varied according to personal preference—"salt and pepper to taste."

Flesh
Burnt sienna
Burnt umber
Titanium white

While there are actually more than six steps in painting a face, this diagram provides a guide that you can follow.

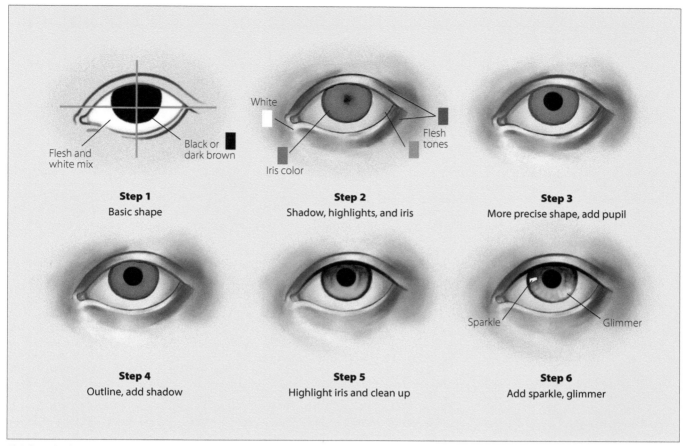

This handy chart shows how to paint eyes in six basic steps. Once you get the hang of it, you can adapt the steps as I have.

Step 1: Define the basic shape of the eye, paint the eye sockets black, paint the whites of the eyes, and leave the iris black.
Step 2: Paint the iris, leaving center of pupil black, and paint shadows.
Step 3: Give eye more precise shape and paint pupil black.
Step 4: Outline and shadow the eye as well as the iris.
Step 5: Add a highlight in the iris' lower quadrant and clean up and sharpen eye area.
Step 6: Add sparkle and glimmer to iris and highlight white.

Next, I moved to the hair, **30**. I styled it with burnt umber acrylic and added a little flesh to it. I faded the top portion with that color, and used a lighter shade of it lower down. Then I stroked the hair with more burnt umber, lightened that, and lightly brushed on highlights.

Only a few small touches remained, **31**. I added shadow and highlights to the crow's feet at the corners of the eyes, as well as to the dimples in the cheeks, the ears, and the upper lip.

I painted the irises Reaper marine teal, the same color as the Special Forces patch, lightened just a little, **32**. I left the pupil black at the center. Then I lightened the marine color a little more and painted a highlight in the lower quadrant of the iris.

Finally, I used a shade of brown to highlight the lips and complete the face.

At this point, you can still go back and use acrylics to clean up little details. If the paint is very thin, and you don't have a lot on your brush, turn the side of your brush to cover a wider area and just touch the high spots or feather out a color.

Wearing the Green Beret

Special Forces berets were a deep green. I have seven of these berets, and the color doesn't vary much at all. There is not a lot of fading or sunbleaching to the fabric. I think Brunswick green is the closest color.

I mixed that color to serve as the base color for the beret. For creating shadows, I added a little black to base color. Then, for highlighting, I mixed a little flesh with the base color. And for superhighlighting, I added a little white to the highlight color. Then to complete the beret, I made a very

thin wash from the base color and went over the beret to blend and unify all the paint layers.

Wearing the beret in the sun will add some shadows to the neck and under the jaw. I used a very thin layer of Vallejo orange brown to lend a bit of shadow to those areas, which also smoothed things out and made the color a little more even.

I was still not quite satisfied. Notice the highlights and shadows on the beret, and take another look at the hair, **33**. I added a real thin wash of burnt umber acrylic over the hair to blend it. You can still see the highlights and shadows, but that wash draws everything closer. Then I added a thin wash of Mars brown oil which produced even more of a unifying effect.

And, finally, with the painting of the beret, we have 1st Lt. George K Sisler, **34**.

Airbrushing skills

This photo shows a Mk1 Shorland Internal Security Vehicle in Syrian markings, which I scratchbuilt back in the mid-'80s. Always one of my favorite models, it is a good example of what you can do with an airbrush, from painting camouflage to weathering. Using a Badger model 100, I airbrushed it with Tamiya paints and then weathered it with Winsor & Newton artist's oils.

Beginning modelers evolve from hand-painting with brushes to painting with spray cans, to ultimately, learning how to airbrush.

After a few unsuccessful rounds with an airbrush, you may be tempted to regress to the "rattle can." But it's better to realize that airbrushing simply takes practice—and to remind yourself that it's often the best way to paint. The No. 1 drawback of spray cans is a lack of control. There is no finesse, no accuracy, and no detailing capabilities. You're very limited. Also, paint from a spray can tends to run and drip because you're putting such a huge amount of paint into a small area. It comes out of the nozzle at 100 mph, and that's hard to control.

With airbrushes—even the bottom of the line "hobby" airbrushes—you have more control and more detailing capabilities. Every modeler wants to find that perfect airbrush—the one that doesn't spit or clog, the one that's the perfect tool.

There's a wide range of airbrushes available, and their prices have quite a range too. You can get something high-end, and that's great if you've got the money. But it's not going to make you a better airbrusher. Practice does that. You don't really need an expensive airbrush until you know why you need an expensive airbrush.

As you learn the craft of airbrushing, you'll encounter your share of problems and frustrations. Remember, it's usually not the airbrush—it's the operator. To operate one successfully, you will need some hand-eye coordination, and a little artistic talent, but most of all you have to practice. And then practice some more.

Airbrush types

There are many different brands and styles of airbrushes, but almost all of them can be classified in two main groups: single-action and double-action. With a single-action airbrush, you set the amount of paint you want to enter the air stream. A trigger controls the amount of air released. On a double-action brush, the trigger controls the amount of paint put into the air stream as well as the amount of air. You push down for air and pull back for paint.

Within both groups, you may find external-mix and internal-mix designs. The external-mix siphons paint from an exterior container. The internal mix is a gravity-feed system with a cup that holds the paint above the body of the airbrush. Once you pour paint in that cup, you have paint in the brush.

I have small hands, so I like a smaller, streamlined airbrush. I also like a double-action, internal-mix airbrush. For me, its advantage is being able to control air and paint with a single finger. It is a little tricky, though, and it takes some coordination. You've got four or five things going at once: holding the model while trying to airbrush; deciding how close to get, with the options of pushing down the trigger to get more air, or pulling back for more paint; and deciding how much pressure to use from the compressor. It's not easy at first.

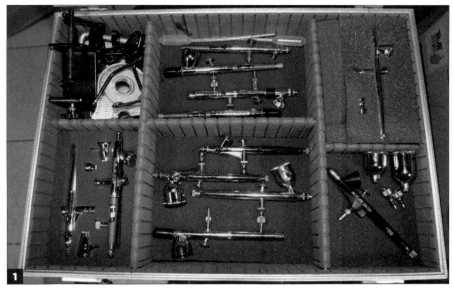

1 When I took the Mrosko Traveling Airbrush Show on the road, it was a load! So, except for my core group, I donated the others for a giveaway at the 2013 Lone Star Figure Show.

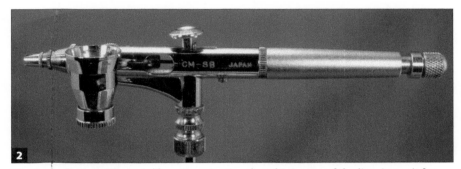

2 The Iwata Custom Micron is like a Ferrari or Lamborghini—top of the line. I save it for special work because I don't want to wear it out. It's a gravity-feed, internal-mix, double-action, precision instrument.

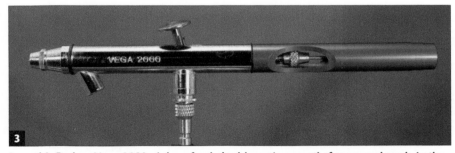

3 I use this Badger Vega 2000, siphon-feed, double-action mostly for general work. In the cutout at the back, you can use the thumbscrew and needle to set the paint amount like a single-action airbrush.

While I prefer the capabilities of a double-action airbrush, I will use a single-action airbrush for covering bigger areas and broader applications, such as applying an overall base coat. (I like to mix it up.)

An overview of airbrushes

At one time, I had 13 or 14 different airbrushes, 1. But now, for the most part, I work with just a few. I use my Tamiya airbrushes for most of my fine detailing. Occasionally, I'll use a Grex, and if I get down to real detail painting, I use a Harder-Steenbeck or an Iwata Micron.

Iwata Custom Micron. To me, this is deluxe model of all airbrushes, 2. It's a great airbrush and has great applications, but I rarely use it anymore. The problem

My Grex XS gravity-feed, double-action, internal-mix is for general, overall applications, usually with acrylics. I like it when I have to work fast since it holds a lot of paint.

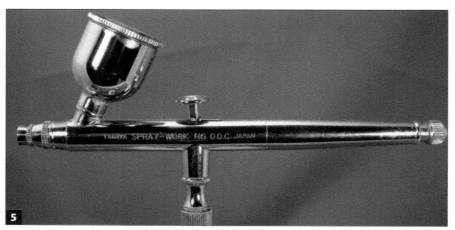

This Tamiya Spray-Work HG gravity-feed, double-action, internal-mix is more than 20 years old and still going. I like its removable color cup.

This Harder & Steenbeck Infinity CR Plus gravity-feed, double-action, internal-mix is a high-end, very precise brush that's great for fine details.

EARLY ADVENTURES IN AIRBRUSHING

My first experience with an airbrush was in the early '70s with one of the Badgers. It had a thin blue air hose, and you hooked it up to an air can. Well, I didn't realize you were supposed to thin the paints or that the can of air would freeze up in a matter of seconds. This first experience with an airbrush was horrible.

Within a year, a buddy of mine showed me the ropes. I was 13 or 14, working at a ballpark shagging baseballs. I saved money all summer to buy two airbrushes. At that time, a Badger 200 was about $40, and the Binks Wren was $50 or $60. I bought both of them, along with hoses and a W. R. Brown compressor. I used those for several years.

In the early '80s, after I got out of the military, I bought a Badger 100 and a Badger 150. Those were like Cadillacs! I used them into the 1990s and have kept them as backups.

Then I hooked up with Tamiya. They sent me several samples of their airbrushes, and I started using them—and I haven't stopped. I'm using the same two airbrushes they first sent me. I've never changed the needles or any other part in them in more than 20 years.

However, I've also used a lot of other airbrushes during that time, not only in my own modeling, but when giving demonstrations and holding seminars. They all have specific strengths that are worth investigating.

I use this brush for general applications of paint on base work and sometimes on models. It's relatively inexpensive and can be found just about anywhere—you can walk into almost any hobby shop or craft store anywhere in the country and find Badger airbrushes, parts, and hoses. They're easy to clean and they have a lifetime guarantee.

Grex XS. I occasionally use the Grex XS, **4**. I like its big paint cup when I have a project going that uses several airbrushes at once. I use it for general, overall application of paints, mainly acrylics.

Tamiya Spray-Work HG. I've been using the same Tamiya Spray-Work HG since 1991, **5**. I use this for about 90 percent of my painting; it's set up and ready

is that if you damage or mess it up somehow, parts are a lot more expensive than they are for other airbrushes. (It's like driving a Ferrari: even an oil filter costs a lot.) So I save it for special projects; I don't want to wear it out.

Badger Vega 2000. I use Badger airbrushes for all-purpose work. They're easy to use, they can take a beating, and they'll suck darned near any kind of paint through. My Badger Vega 2000 is a siphon-feed, double-action airbrush, **3**.

to go at all times. The removable color cup is an advantage, and you can use a bigger one if you want. I haven't changed or replaced a single part. I've dropped it, I've banged it up—you can tell by looking at it. It's a gravity-fed, double-action, internal-mix airbrush.

Harder & Steenbeck Infinity CR Plus. This is a fantastic airbrush. It's a little more expensive than the average, but it's a well-made, fine detailing brush, **6**. It is great with a distance cap on it, **7**. The halo helps you maintain a constant distance, which is great for painting lines or edges where consistency is essential.

Badger Sotar 20/20. The Badger Sotar 20/20 has fantastic capabilities for detail painting, but you've got to keep it clean, **8**. It's a little finicky that way.

I consider the Infinity and the Sotar equal to the Iwata Micron except for price. You can have a few of these for the price of a Micron. They're all well-made airbrushes.

Sata Graph 4B. I really like the Sata Graph 4B, **9**. It features a little slot at the tip of the brush called a crown tip. When you get close to something, the opening lets air through so paint doesn't get backed up against the nozzle. Otherwise, that feedback can cause a lot of trouble, like overspray or splattering. You can get really close and paint with precision and not worry about it blowing back. This brush is actually an automotive detailing airbrush, but it is inexpensive and works well.

Compressors

An airbrush can't function without pressurized air. Some people use tanks of nitrogen or CO_2, but the setup and refills can be complex and a little pricey, so most people use a compressor as their air source. There are many available, and they range from less than $100 to thousands of dollars.

The determining factors in choosing a compressor are steady pressure, peripheral equipment, such as a regulator and moisture trap, and noise. You can get an inexpensive and powerful compressor at any hardware or home improvement store, but it might be noisy enough to draw complaints.

At home, I use a Super Silent Silentaire, **10**. It's terrific but expensive. All compressors, even expensive ones, ooze a little

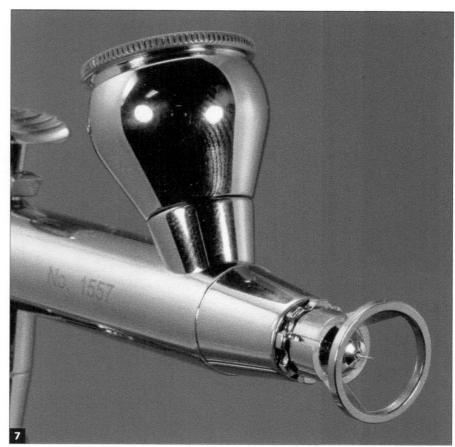

7

A distance cap at the tip of the airbrush helps when consistency—repeatable results—is critical.

8

A Badger Sotar 20/20 gravity-feed, double-action, internal-mix is a great detailing brush, but you need to take extra care cleaning it if you want it to work as it should.

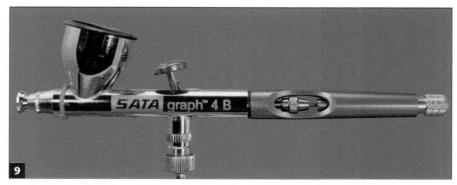

9

I really like the Sata Graph 4B, gravity-feed, double-action, internal-mix. It has a crown tip that vents air pressure and keeps the air/paint mix from billowing when you're working close.

10

11

This Super Silentaire 50 compressor is quiet and rock-solid. Its air-storage tank (foreground) holds a ready supply of compressed air, preventing pulsation to keep the air stream constant.

The Badger TC910 is very reliable, affordable, compact, and relatively quiet. You don't see it here, but it also has an air-storage tank to prevent pulsation.

12

13

I take this Grex when I'm traveling, and it's a handy little guy. See that regulator? A lot of small compressors don't have one.

I use this big Husky for my resin-casting setup and for airbrushing if need be.

lubricant, so I made an oil pan (cardboard lined with heavy-duty ⅛" sheet styrene) to set it in, which you can see in the photo. It cuts down on the mess at my workbench.

For my backup compressor, and when I travel for demonstrations, I use a Badger TC910, **11**. It's not silent, but it's pretty quiet and provides a steady flow, with no pulsing, and it's relatively inexpensive.

If I have to fly, I take a Grex ⅛-horsepower portable, piston compressor, **12**. It's light and tight, and great for traveling. It pulses a little bit but not bad, and, unlike

a lot of similar-sized compressors, it has an air regulator.

If all else fails, I always have my big ol' Husky compressor, **13**. It's a monster! And to be honest, as far as affordability, you can't go wrong with a compressor like this—but it's pretty loud! With this compressor, you don't have to worry about any condensation, moisture buildup, or anything like that. It's the same one I use for all my resin casting.

I like quick-disconnect joins on all my hoses. You can change brushes instantly, and you don't have to worry about cross-

threading or stripping the connectors. And I prefer compressors that have a standard ¼" hookup, which makes it a lot easier to find parts when you need them or if you want to do a splitter and run two airbrushes at the same time, **14**.

At times, I'll have two stands set up, for holding four airbrushes. If you're going to use different colors, this makes it easier than having to clean a brush between applications. I'm able to switch colors on the fly because I make the paint very thin and spray at high pressure—30-60psi—so it dries very quickly.

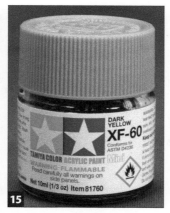

15 Tamiya is one of the best airbrush paints for modeling. It doesn't have the hard, shell-like finish of traditional enamels, and it gives great coverage.

16 I use FolkArt acrylic for hand-painting or airbrushing. It's pretty thick; I thin it 3 parts thinner to 1 part paint.

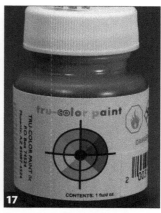

17 Tru-Color is thin, airbrushes well, and dries tough. And the color range includes just about anything you need!

14 Most of the time I have two airbrushes set up, one for enamels or lacquers, and the other for acrylics. The Tamiya brush stands are nice for that.

Types of paint

I prefer to paint with acrylics. I was introduced to acrylics in 1990, and I've never gone back. My choice of brands is as much by habit as anything. I use what I'm comfortable with, and I use what works. If something doesn't work, I pitch it and move on.

I mostly use Tamiya acrylics, **15**. I like the performance of Tamiya paint. You can cut it thin and still get nice coverage, it has good texture, and the smell won't run anyone out of the house. If you screw something up, you can take it to a sink, spray it with Windex, and the paint will come right off.

Of course there are many other good paints. I like painting with FolkArt, an acrylic enamel usually known as a craft paint, **16**. It sprays well and it's inexpensive. A similar paint that also works well is Delta Ceramcoat. You can get these brands at craft stores, discount stores, and hobby shops for half or less of what scale-modeling brands cost.

I recently discovered a paint line out of Phoenix called Tru-Color, **17**. It's model railroad oriented and has the best color ranges I've seen. You can get olive drab, forest green, and tons of military colors. They may just have different names. I picked out a color called big sky blue, that's perfect for UN blue. There are 250

colors to mix and match. The paints flow well and they're fantastic for airbrushing.

Paint sets for certain types of vehicles or a specific theater of operations, such as AK Interactive's Iraq and Afghanistan set of acrylics, can make your life easier, **18**. The colors are matched to Federal Standard or RAL colors, even faded a little for scale effect. You don't have to thin them much, either—they are made for airbrushing. Nothing could be easier.

For metallics, the best line is Gunze Sangyo Mr. Metal Color, **19**; nothing else is even close. And every once in a while, I'll dip into the regular Gunze Sangyo acrylic paints, which are hard to find in the U.S. (Gunze Sangyo's acrylic line has been discontinued for years here and is currently not being imported.)

Speaking of scarcity, I still have a lot of Aeromaster paints, **20**. It's not being made anymore. I have some left and I love the colors. It's still my favorite paint for aircraft.

But most of what I do are figures and armor. For that, you need a dead-flat finish. I use Testors Dullcote, the ultimate flat clear, **21**. It's available in spray cans but I buy it in the bottle and thin it 1:1 with lacquer thinner. You have to keep an eye on it, though, because it can yellow. If you look at the bottle and see a deep mustard color, don't use it. You want to use it when it looks white and cloudy. Another thing about Dullcote: Every once in a while it will turn your model white, like a glaze. If that happens, overspray it with lacquer. That will clear it up.

Practice exercises

If you want to be a good airbrusher, you have to practice. Get a piece of cardboard—any color—and practice spraying different diameters of airflow. Start out slow and see if you can just do a straight, thin line, **22**. Then do a little thicker line, and work your way up until you're airbrushing wide open.

Also work on your control. Learn the spray patterns and what causes the airbrush to spit. Experiment with proximity, **23**. The closer you are, the thinner the paint and the finer the line you'll be able to paint. Get as close as you can. Use the pinky finger on your other hand as a gauge. Lay it right on the cardboard and get the airbrush right alongside it. Get to that distance and see what it takes to spray.

Most of the airbrushes I use have a crown tip on them. This tip prevents air backup, so you don't have that blast coming in and messing things up, pushing your paint away from where you're aiming it, or causing paint to build up on the lip where it can spit. Practice that.

Another suggestion, which may sound kind of funny, is to play airbrush tic-tac-toe. Spray the crosshatch, then paint the circles and Xs in the spaces, staying inside the lines. Do it as cleanly as you can. At first, just try to put them in the squares. You'll be surprised how that will improve your aim.

Also, practice painting figure 8s. I do continuous figure 8s. I start wide and dial

A set of premixed colors takes the guesswork out of matching military colors. Add a dab of thinner, and it's pretty close to being airbrush-ready right out of the bottle.

19 Gunze Sangyo Mr. Metal Color are wonderful paints for metal finishes on aircraft models.

20 Aeromaster is an out-of-production line that people still hoard; it's my favorite paint for aircraft.

21 Dullcote is the go-to flat clear. When you need to knock the shine off a model, Dullcote lives up to its name.

it down until the lines are fine. The larger they are, the wider spray pattern I use; as I reduce the size, I go down to a hairline paint stream.

Learn how to push the trigger down and start the paint off the model. That way, if there's any spitting, it happens away from the model. Start your stroke and follow completely through. Start off the model at one end, carry through to the other end, and stop only after you're off the model again. Gaining that little bit of control will take you a long way toward the desired results.

Paints and your airbrush

Most modelers don't work with multiple airbrushes like I do. But I'm always modeling, so my airbrushes are set up and ready

to go at all times. I keep alcohol in them between sessions. I'll pick up an airbrush and spray out what little alcohol might be in it. Then I strain and add the paint, which is already thinned.

TIP: Some people use Windex as an all-purpose cleaner. But Windex and other ammonia-based cleaners can etch the metal finish on parts inside your airbrush.

When I'm through, I'll turn the brush over and dump the paint back in its container. Then I'll spray some more alcohol through the brush to clean it out, wipe it down, spray a little lacquer thinner through it, and add a little more alcohol so the airbrush is totally cleaned.

Then you're ready to switch colors. Put

the next color in, spray a little bit on a piece of cardboard just to make sure the brush has all the cleaning solutions out of it, and you're set to go.

The only exception to my usual routine is with certain colors (like red) when you're going to a lighter color such as white. Make sure you have the airbrush clean because there will be some bleeding. I don't care how well you think you've cleaned that airbrush, some paint will come out.

And then there is white. It always has little chunks of pigment in it somewhere, so you often get a little bit of spitting. You may have used white, cleaned the brush, but, then later on, I don't know where it comes from, you'll be painting something blue, red, or green, and all of a sudden, you'll get little white bits of paint. It has a way of hiding until later. Yellow does that as well.

TIP: When using yellow, white, or red—make sure you *really* clean that airbrush.

You may have similar trouble using Testors Dullcote. You've got to clean your brush carefully after using it, or you'll get little specks of white, hardened Dullcote slung onto your model. Also, you need to thin it well when using it.

Even if you don't use multiple airbrushes at one time, it can really help to have at least a couple set aside for different applications—for example, one for enamels or lacquers and another for acrylics. I do not spray metallics with the same airbrush I use for another paint. It is hard to get metallics out of your airbrush. Just like white, somehow you'll have some metallic flake come through later on. (I call these bits meteors since they come flying out of nowhere.)

Because I hardly ever do detail painting with it, I'll use my Badger for metallic paint, usually for overall applications to color ammunition, aircraft wings, and the like. Along with the airbrush, I keep the thinners—anything that has to do with metallics—off to one side so I know I won't grab the wrong airbrush. Metallics are unforgiving.

If I'm spraying metallics, I make sure to keep the rest of the model covered up and away from the spraying area. Otherwise, those meteors will float through the air and land on something they shouldn't.

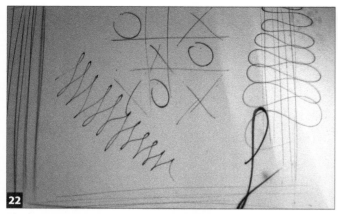

The best way to avoid making a mistake with a model is to practice without the model. Airbrush lines of different weights and varying thicknesses or spray tight designs freehand. Improve your accuracy with a game of tic-tac-toe (you'll always win).

You know you have control of the airbrush when you can paint from this distance without making a mess. It's a combination of the right paint/thinner ratio, correct pressure, and using the right amount of paint at that pressure.

The pressure's on

I generally spray at 30–60psi. That's usually higher than most modelers use. But I've learned over the years that the higher the pressure, the thinner the paint, and the finer the line I can spray. At this pressure, I also have less overspray or *orange peeling*. (Orange peel is a slightly bumpy surface that results from paint piling up erratically on the surface.)

I know some modelers spray at 12–15psi, but I find at that pressure, you get more spitting and orange peeling. The paint just drools out of the brush. At the higher pressure, the paint is being forced out, and you're putting it where you want it. To me, it's a lot easier spraying at a higher pressure. But to do so, you have to have the paint mixture right, and put the paint on in thin coats. You can always build up layers and add more paint. But it's a lot tougher to take it off.

The lowest pressure I'll use is 20psi, and that's very rare. I usually use it in the late stages of a project when I want to avoid blowing things off a model. These are times when I have a model that I thought was finished, and I'll see something that's just not right. I'll go back and maybe touch something up, or add a little shadow or some weathering.

More about proximity

When I'm doing a general application, like putting a base coat on a model, I spray 4"–8" away. There are times, depending on the shape of the model, where you have to get a little closer to shoot into an overhang or an undercut.

When I do my detail painting—it all depends on what it is, camouflage or fine lines—I get as close as I can. I'll lay a finger on the surface and airbrush from no farther away than that (as demonstrated in photo **23**).

If you paint that close, make sure your hands are clean. I keep alcohol, Windex, and a roll of paper towels close by and continually clean my hands when airbrushing.

Handling models

When touching a model, you just have to keep your hands clean. I hate seeing a greasy finger mark on a model. You can't get rid of it. You can try to lightly sand it or rub it out and then go back over with Dullcote or whatever to make the sheen match again. But usually you just can't get rid of it.

However, I'm not one of these guys that likes modeling in gloves. I don't like touching the model with latex gloves. I do use them for casting resin, but that's to keep the resin off my fingers—not to keep my fingers off the resin. I like to be able to feel the model. I'm closer to it that way. I don't get the same feeling wearing gloves. I'd rather touch the model, to know how much pressure I can put on it while I'm holding it. I don't like to use cotton gloves either. I've seen modelers snag an antenna or a pitot tube and snap it off while wearing cotton gloves; that wouldn't happen otherwise.

One of the handiest tools I have for painting is a custom-made painting stand, **24**. A fellow up in Michigan made this

This is my custom-made paint stand. I use it all the time. I can hold it or set it down and have both hands free. (If you're a hardware-store guy, you can likely build one of your own.)

TROUBLESHOOTING YOUR AIRBRUSH

If you'e having trouble airbrushing, most likely the problem is related to the paint, moisture, or airflow.

Paint problems

THICKNESS
Often, the paint is just too thick. It's globbing up, it's not spraying, or you can't get it through the nozzle. Practice with your paints as well as your airbrush. Learn how to thin paints so you get the proper consistency. If you thin your paint too much, it will splatter and run.

If you have a siphon-fed airbrush, the tube coming out of the bottle may suck up goo that makes its way into your airbrush. Make sure to use the correct thinner for your paint. There are many things you can't cut acrylics with, and there are different types of acrylics. (I've added the wrong thinner and turned some paints to gel.) That's why the paint manufacturer's thinner is the first choice; it is formulated for that particular paint.

But you can cut most acrylics with lacquer thinner. Pigment is pigment; it doesn't matter if the suspension is lacquer, enamel, or acrylic—pigment is the same. I usually use acrylic paint thinned with 91 percent isopropyl alcohol.

STRAINING
If you have paint that's already thinned, don't just dump it into the reservoir and start spraying. Make sure you stir the paint. I haven't had too much trouble with Tamiya paints, but if you use any others, you should strain the paint too.

You can strain it and then thin it, or vice versa, but be sure to strain it. I don't know how, but you'll find lint, dust, and metal shavings. I have no idea where these particles come from, but they're reason enough to strain the paint!

Use a small, wire-mesh strainer, like one you would find among cooking supplies. Run the paint through the strainer to get the big clumps out, and then take a blunt instrument, such as a wood dowel, and push the chunks of pigment through the strainer. You want to keep as much pigment as possible. Then, thin the paint and strain it again. That way, you retain as much of the pigment as possible.

For a final fine-straining, take a swatch of pantyhose and tie it around the mesh strainer. Pour the paint through and then it's ready for airbrushing!

Moisture problems

Occasionally, you may have trouble with condensation in your air line. The worst time to airbrush is during hot summer afternoons filled with high humidity.

You can buy an inline moisture trap, but they don't always work. If you do install one, put it on the very last hookup coming off the compressor. That's what you should connect your hose to. And if you're that concerned, you can get two and hook them back to back.

If you have a CO_2 tank, you'll never have issues with water in the line, but that's kind of an expensive route to go. With the compressors I use at home, I don't have much of a problem with water in the line. But if I travel to do a seminar or demonstration, I use a smaller compressor, and I do use a moisture trap with it. Some smaller compressors without a built-in moisture trap can spit like crazy.

If a bit of water does spit out and lands on your model, first stop spraying the paint. Then using air only, aim your airbrush at the moisture and dry it off. I've had that happen with every type of paint I've ever used, acrylic or enamel. Remain calm—just keep the air on it and dry it right away.

Airflow problems

PROPER AIRFLOW
Obtaining the proper airflow can be problematic. Everything is air-propelled. First, make sure there are no restrictions. Also, check that all connections are good throughout the airbrush and that everything is tightened properly and not leaking.

AIR BUT NO PAINT
If you're getting air but no paint, it may be that the needle is not moving back and forth all the way. Without forcing it, make sure the needle is pushed all the way forward. Also make sure your paint reservoir is attached properly and that any connections in a siphon-fed setup are all nice and snug. Some paint reservoirs have little vent holes to allow airflow. If one of those is clogged, the paint won't flow.

I prefer gravity-feed designs, in which the paint cup simply drains into the airbrush. What you put in comes out one way or the other, either through the tip of the airbrush or all over your hand if you tip it over accidentally.

---

odd-looking thing for me, and I use it all the time. It's about 7" tall and has a collet on the end, so you can chuck a dowel or whatever you rig to a piece to hold it for painting. It's nice and heavy, so it won't tip or blow over when airbrushing. It has a nice, thick shaft so I have a good grip if I want to hold it up. After a No. 11 hobby knife, Tamiya cutters, and sanding sticks, this is the most-used tool on my workbench. (There's more about these tools in the Appendix.) Unfortunately, stands like this are not for sale, but you could go to a hardware store and find the parts to put something like it together.

Cleaning your airbrush
Some people break the airbrush down after every session to clean it. I don't think that's necessary. In fact, you wear out the airbrush by doing that. You also risk damaging the needle or losing parts. And it's very easy to cross-thread or strip some of those little internal components. I break down an airbrush about once a year and do a thorough cleaning.

With the airbrushing methods I've developed, I don't have to do more than that. At the end of each day I use an airbrush, I spray lacquer thinner through it, wipe out the tip, wipe out the cup, and

pull the needle and wipe it down. Then I put some Medea Super Lube on the needle and put it back through.

I don't recommend taking everything apart and soaking it in lacquer thinner for long periods either. By doing that, you damage the grommets and washers and etch the metal.

If you do break it down, clean it, put it back together, rinse with alcohol, and that's it. I have a little set of cleaning brushes that work great, but don't overdo it. The harder you scrub, the more of the metal finish you will wear away. Keep it simple.

This USMC M1A1 (Common Heavy) tank is loaded with far more parts than came in the kit. You can shop the aftermarket for accessories, but resin casting is a great way to make copies of parts or make new ones. This Abrams is now ready to roll into action in Operation Iraqi Freedom.

6

Resin casting

Resin has been used for years in various industries, for everything from Detroit autos to knick-knacks. Bakelite was one of the first synthetic plastics in the early 20th century, and it was used to manufacture countless products, including telephones, radios, rifle stocks, pistol grips, and even toy train accessories. For the general scale modeling community, resin casting rose in popularity in the mid-1980s. Verlinden introduced casting to the military modeling market around 1985.

Resins can be soft and flexible or hard and clear. Polyester resin has durability and strength, but you need a band saw and a power sander to work it. I use polyurethane resin because it's much easier to carve, sand, and clean.

1 Here's the whole resin-casting setup, all nice and clean (for now). On the top shelf, the pressure pot is on the left, the vacuum chamber is in the center, and the vacuum pump is on the right. Silicone and resin components are next to the pressure pot. The bottom shelf contains rubber gloves, cups, and mixing containers.

2 The Welch vacuum pump (model no. 1400) on the right is an industrial-strength piece of equipment, but it runs on 110 volts. You can buy a rebuilt one for about $1,500. On the left is a vacuum chamber, or degassing station, made by JB Eliminator.

The casting process

For the Abrams project shown in this chapter, I needed more parts than what the kit supplied, so I cast them in resin. Although I use professional casting equipment, you can use the information provided to duplicate parts or create new ones. If you have a premade part, you can make additional copies of it. You can use one or more premade parts to make a different casting, or you can sculpt your own master.

If you've ever had a tooth crowned, you've seen the casting process. The dentist makes a rubbery mold from room-temperature vulcanizing (RTV) silicone

and then pours dental resin in the mold to form the new crown. I'll describe the essence of the process, and you'll see the various considerations that go into making the best castings you can.

Equipment and materials

Keep in mind, I use a professional resin-casting setup, which, with an air compressor and various fittings, is about $2,500 worth of equipment, **1**. That may seem expensive, but it's not a huge investment if you want to get more serious about the hobby and cast parts for your modeling projects. But you don't necessarily need

all the pressurizing and depressurizing equipment to cast resin or buy your materials in 5-gallon quantities.

I use a light industrial vacuum pump and vacuum chamber for depressurizing the silicone and resin, **2**. The depressurizing takes the air bubbles, which can distort and even ruin a piece, out of the poured silicone and resin.

Another handy piece of equipment is a pressure pot, **3**. You want your parts to have fine detail with sharp, crisp edges. Assuming you have a good master part and a good mold, the resin should conform to every little ridge and fold of the mold. Forc-

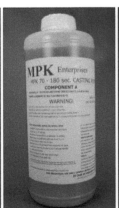

3 Housepainters call it a paint pot, but I call it a pressure pot. (The 2.5 gallon pot is available at Sears.) I'll run it anywhere from 25–80psi. The yellow handle on the brass fitting is the pressure release. You have to release the pressure first before opening that pot.

4 I get my materials from MPK Enterprises, a great supplier for modelers, run by Michael P. Knott. From left is molding silicone (no. 2125), silicone catalyst (blue), resin (MPK-70, part A), and resin hardener (MPK-70, part B).

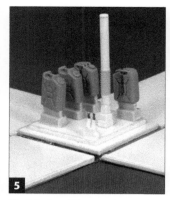

5 First, I glued the master parts to pour plugs. Then I glued them to a platform that forms a reservoir in what becomes the top of the mold when the silicone cures.

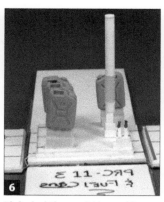

6 I labeled the mold by writing backwards on the inside of the box with a felt-tip pen; the ink will then transfer to the mold.

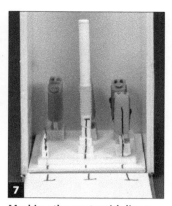

7 Marking the parts with lines guided me as I cut the cured mold open. Marks on the side of the box transferred to the sides of the mold showed me where to stop cutting.

8 With the box on its side, you can see the parts secured to the bottom plate. The box is sealed with packing tape and ready for the silicone.

ing the air out of the mold and the resin into it is key. That's where the pressure pot comes in. Mine is actually a paint pot for a house spray-painting system. I put a mold full of resin in the pressure pot to force the resin farther into the mold, which produces the fine details you are looking for.

Other necessary equipment you may already have includes safety glasses, rubber gloves, plastic cups, mixing containers, and a small scale.

Tip: Always wear safety glasses and rubber gloves throughout this process. Resin in the eyes means a painful trip to the emergency room for an eye wash!

You only need a few materials for casting your own parts, **4**. For making the molds, you need RTV silicone and a catalyst. I use a medium-strength silicone and catalyst. For casting the parts, I use a two-part polyurethane resin that is strong and has a slight flex to it.

Boxing the masters

Casting begins with making the master parts. I made several 5-gallon water containers, two 5-gallon gas cans, and a few parts for a large custom-made PRC-113 antenna (turned on a lathe by my buddy Charlie Pritchett). Cast copies of all these parts went on my Abrams.

The first step is gluing the parts to a sprue or a pour plug, **5**. Not actually part of the castings, think of the pour plugs as handles. They can be made of chunks of styrene.

Before gluing the master parts to their plugs, I coated them with Testors Dullcote, a flat, clear lacquer. The flat finish works better than a glossy one. If you use a glossy-finished master part, the duplicates will come out glossy. And if the master part is scratched, you're going to see those scratches on the copies because the silicone duplicates exactly what you put in the mold box. Parts with a flat finish don't show scratches as readily, and they take paint better than parts with a shiny finish.

I made the mold box from .125" styrene sheet that I got from Cope Plastics. The styrene has a smooth finish that the silicone won't stick to. I built the mold box with four sides and a bottom plate. A smaller plate rest on top of the bottom plate to create a reservoir on what will become the top of the mold after the silicone cures. Later, when the resin is poured, that reservoir catches any overflow.

I attached the reservoir plate to the bottom plate with packing tape, lightly roughed up the surface, and then super glued the master parts to it. You want to go easy with the glue, so later, when it's time to extract the parts from the mold, those parts will easily snap away from the plastic. But to make sure they are secure, I applied a little super glue accelerator. (A *floater*, a piece that comes loose during the molding process, can ruin your mold—and your day).

I used a Sharpie felt-tip pen to label the mold (Blue seems to work best). I wrote the title backwards on the inside surface of the box, and some of the ink transfers to the silicone mold during the process, **6**.

Other marks helped guide me when I cut open the mold to extract the masters, **7**. Marks on the parts and on the outside of the mold indicated where to stop cutting the cured silicone around the molding cavity. Then I sealed the box with packing tape. If I have more than one mold going, I'll label the outside of the box too. When the box is sealed shut, you're ready to pour the silicone, **8**.

Pouring the silicone mold

I measure everything in grams. (I used to weigh everything on a really nice expensive electronic scale, but since they are easily ruined, I bought a postal scale for about $40 at an office supply store.) I poured in the silicone and added 10 percent catalyst, **9**.

LEARNING TO CAST

I learned about resin casting for modeling in the late 1970s from a dentist in Illinois who liked to use it for making model parts. I'd never heard of it before, and I thought, "This is great! He's making his own parts!" When I got a better grip on what it was all about, I started experimenting with the process. Eventually, I went to work for Kirin Models (formerly a subsidiary of Dragon) in 1991 as a patternmaker and moldmaker. I'd make the patterns, box the molds, pour in the rubber, and remove the parts. That was not only my introduction to the industry, it was also the beginning of my professional modeling.

9 After I put a paper towel on the scale to protect it, I set the pail on it, zeroed the scale, and then poured the silicone. Here, I'm adding the blue catalyst.

10 I like using a wide straightedge as a stir tool because I can scrape the side of the bucket with it. I stir in a figure-8 pattern to mix the silicone and catalyst thoroughly.

11 Even with a gentle stirring, the silicone has some bubbles in it—but not for long.

12 I set the pail of silicone in the vacuum chamber to pull out the bubbles. This part of the process can get a little messy.

13 After getting rid of the bubbles, pouring the silicone in a thin stream prevents air from being reintroducing into the mixture. Pouring from higher up also prevents bubbles.

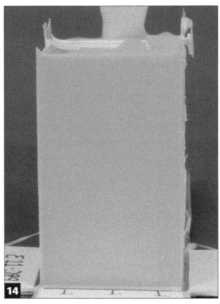

14 After about four hours, I cut open the box and pulled it away from the cured silicone. I then sliced off ragged edges and scraps so they wouldn't snag and possibly damage the mold.

15 There's the reservoir. A couple of pour plugs have come loose, but I can still retrieve their parts.

SUPPLIERS
- **Vacuum pump and chamber**
  Avac Industries, avac.com
- **Molding silicone and casting resin**
  MPK Enterprises, hobbysilicone.com
- **Sheet plastic**
  Cope Plastics, copeplastics.com
- **Pressure pot**
  Sears, sears.com
- **Applicator bottles,**
  Sally's Beauty Supply,
  sallybeauty.com

Then I stirred it thoroughly, yet gently, with a metal ruler, **10**.

The 4-hour catalyst provides a "quick set," as silicone goes. After thorough mixing, the silicone had some bubbles in it, **11**. I put the pail of silicone in the vacuum chamber, sealed it, and fired up the vacuum pump, **12**.

As the vacuum chamber evacuates, the silicone rises in the pail, gets near the top, and then suddenly deflates. (It looks like a cake gone bad in the oven.) Sometimes you have to repeat this step

three or four times to get all the air out.

I removed the pail from the chamber and poured the silicone into the mold box in a slow, thin stream to avoid introducing air, **13**. Then, it was back into the vacuum chamber for the mold to remove as much air out as possible.

TIP: If you don't want to use all this casting equipment, you can still get a good mold without all the pressurization. Pour the silicone from about 24" above the mold box to get rid of the air bubbles.

16

With the cuts made, gently pry them open to extract the master parts. Once that's done, reseal the mold with tape, being careful to align the inner edges of the mold cavity to avoid big mold lines (and extra work). Then you're ready to pour the resin into it.

17

Following the faint marks on the outside of the mold, cut through to the parts inside. The less you have to cut, the more you can preserve the integrity of the mold.

18

I poured equal parts of the catalyst and resin, 10 grams each, after weighing it to make sure the amounts were more accurate.

19

My resin agitator is a former spatula handle. I mixed the resin vigorously and rapidly since it cures in three minutes.

20

A syringe works great for drawing the resin up out of the cup and injecting it in the mold.

21

When injecting the mold with resin, go slowly. A sudden burp of air from the mold can expel resin, so stand back and wear eye protection at all times.

About four hours later, I checked the mold. If the silicone feels tacky or sticky, it's not totally cured. Let it cure longer. (Weather and humidity have a direct effect on both silicone and resin curing.) When the silicone was cured, I cut the box open, **14**. Before much more handling, I carefully trimmed off the rough edges with a hobby knife to prevent them from snagging on something and tearing the mold.

Next, I pulled away the box and the end plate to reveal the reservoir, **15**. A few of the master parts came loose from their pour plugs and were still inside the mold,

which was OK. The parts are easier to remove that way.

Now comes the tricky part: cutting the mold open to remove the master parts, **16**. To do so, I followed the faint marks on the silicone that transferred from the box. When you do, move the knife lightly along the path of the part—you can tell when you hit the part. You don't want to slice the part, just lightly trace the side of it. As I cut, and after the cut was made, **17**, I gently spread it open with my fingers to see the markings on the part. Easy does it! This takes a lot of practice. I've been doing this for 20 years, and I've made my share

of mistakes. When the parts are out, seal the mold back up with tape and restore it to its proper shape.

Pouring the resin

Back at the scale, I put the cup on, zeroed out the scale, set it on grams, and poured 10 grams of catalyst. I poured the catalyst, Part B, first. If you pour a little less catalyst, the resin is still going to cure, just slower. That's better than having too little resin. Next, I poured 10 grams of Part A, the yellow resin, using an applicator bottle from Sally's Beauty Supply, **18**. These bottles have tops that stay on! (The last thing you

22

I left excess resin in the reservoir to be sure there was plenty inside the mold. Then the mold went back in the vacuum chamber.

23

After being removed from the vacuum chamber, the resin in the reservoir was full of tiny air bubbles pulled from within the mold.

24

Using a spatula, I skimmed off the excess resin so the parts were easier to extract individually.

25

I placed the mold into the pressure pot. At 80psi the resin is forced deeper into the mold.

26

Going up! The pressure builds gradually to 80psi so air doesn't rush into the pot too abruptly and tip over the mold. At the same time, the resin is curing. That's why I have all my tools lying around the pot. When you have a 3-minute cure, you've got to throw it down and go!

want—and it has happened to me—is to squeeze the bottle and have the top pop off.)

So now I had 20 grams of resin ready for the next step. For this project, I was using a resin that cured in three minutes, so I had to keep moving.

I use different resins for different projects. In addition to a 3-minute resin, I also have resins that cure in 5, 8, or 12 minutes. To give yourself more time, you can refrigerate one or both parts of the two-part resin, which will give you about twice the working time.

I stirred the resin like heck, clockwise and then counterclockwise, 20–30 turns each, and finished with a few more clockwise strokes, **19**. Then I pulled the resin

from the cup with a Monoject 412 syringe, **20**. For easier use, I cut the syringe tip about ¼" to widen its opening. Careful: If you pull back too far on the plunger, it could be a resin splash disaster.

I then slowly injected the resin into the mold to avoid splattering, **21**. As air is forced out of the syringe, resin can suddenly squirt from the mold. Stand back and, as always, be sure to wear eye protection. While injecting the resin, I usually set the mold on one of those black plastic trays used in a grocery store deli department for salads and other foods. For some reason, this resin doesn't stick to that plastic. So if I spill a little resin on the tray, I just let it dry, flex the tray, and pop the resin right off.

After the resin was poured and the reservoir filled, the mold was ready for the vacuum chamber, **22**. I left extra resin in the reservoir so, if the vacuum chamber draws air out of the mold, there would still be plenty of resin in the casting.

After taking the mold out of the vacuum chamber, you'll see tiny bubbles, almost like carbonation, on top of the mold, **23**. The bubbles indicate how much air has been pulled out of the mold.

I took a spatula and skimmed the excess resin into a spare cup, **24**. Scooping off the excess makes it easier to pull the tape off and remove those parts from the mold later. If you had a solid block of resin, you'd have to tear up the mold and risk breaking the castings to get the parts loose.

27

You can see how the pressure has pushed resin into the mold. There's even a little "short-shot" as the resin is short of the very top of the mold, but it is not enough to spoil the pieces.

28

I snipped away excess resin with a sprue clippers (Tamiya Craft Tools 74035 sharp-pointed side cutters) and then removed the sealing tape and gently pried the mold open to extract the castings.

29

The first piece came out of the mold and was looking good.

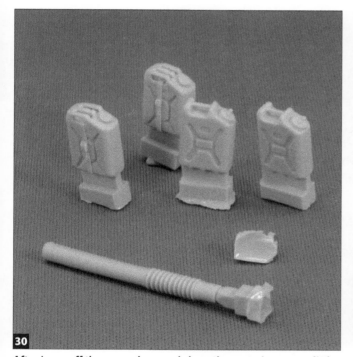

30

After I saw off the pour plugs and clean the cast pieces up a little, they'll be ready to install on the Abrams.

31

The antenna and gas cans, as well as several other resin-cast items, have been added to the tank. All the extra parts add up to make a more detailed model.

Now the mold went into the pressure tank, **25**. I put the lid on and tightened it down. I built the pressure by letting the air in slowly. Otherwise, the incoming air can tip the mold over and blow the resin right out of the mold. It probably takes 10–20 seconds to put the air and get the pressure up to 80psi, **26**.

Demolding

The pressure pot pushed the resin into the mold and left a little "short-shot," **27**, but it

was still within acceptable parameters for personal use. I cut away the tape sealing the mold and used a sprue clipper to snip away excess resin, **28**.

To extract a casting from the mold, part the silicone and very slowly and carefully pull it out. If you try to yank it out, you'll rip the mold. It's a four-finger process. I spread the rubber with two fingers on one hand and eased the first part, a modern-style fuel can, out with two fingers on my other hand, **29**.

I carefully took the rest of the castings out of the mold, and they looked mighty clean, **30**. After a little trimming, they were ready to detail my Abrams tank and make it look like it belongs in the field, **31**.

My system optimizes the resin-casting process. But you don't need all this equipment to cast resin. If you can build simply, mix well, and pour slowly, you can simply and effectively make your own resin castings.

7

The Way of the Rabbit

"The Way of the Rabbit" tells the story of four American Rangers racing through France on an abandoned Kettenkrad, a peculiar German tracked motorcycle. The Dragon 1/35 scale Kettenkrad pulls an infantry cart from Bronco. The groundwork is made of sheet styrene, vacuum-formed and resin stonework, epoxy resin water—and a lot of paint that turned plastic and resin into stone.

After D-Day, June 6, 1944, it would be two months before the Allies broke out of Normandy. When the Germans retreated, they left behind more than 2,000 vehicles. Among these would have been a few *Kettenkraftrads* (*Kettenkrad* for short). These odd tracked motorcycles served as light tractors for airborne and infantry troops, and sometimes as gun tractors or runway tugs for aircraft.

Wartime photos show grinning GIs astride German motorcycles and Kettenkrads. But my inspiration for this scene came from the movie *Saving Private Ryan*, in which American soldiers take a wild ride on a Kettenkrad to lure German tanks into an ambush. As the Germans approach, Tom Hanks' character orders his men to "get on the rabbit," referring to it as a hunting quarry.

1

After deciding on a bilevel base and determining the dimensions, I cut 1" particle board to serve as subflooring with two pieces stacked for the upper level.

2

A street on the upper level will rest on six risers cut from .125" sheet styrene. They're numbered because each is a slightly different height, due to the slight irregularities in the particle-board surface. Each riser will fit in the spot where they were measured.

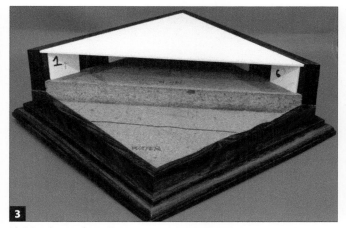

3

I laid a sheet of .125" styrene on the risers to act as a level and supporting underlayment for the street surface.

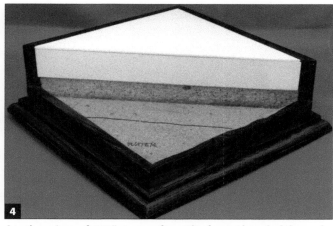

4

Another piece of .125" styrene faces the front. I beveled the ends so it fit against the walnut walls.

The Americans won the ensuing skirmish but were decimated. I didn't want that. I wanted GIs on a Kettenkrad cruising through southern France in late summer 1944. Still, I called my vignette "The Way of the Rabbit."

A wartime diorama or a vignette doesn't always have to be covered with wreckage. Often, when modelers add rubble, they actually don't do enough of it. In buildings that have been bombed, numerous floors have been knocked down. Modelers may build a scene where the rubble has been pushed aside, but that's not how it was.

I wanted to show a sliver of a non-scorched portion of France. Although there was widespread devastation throughout the country, some places were relatively untouched. So why not model clean, pristine street surfaces? Eventually, my plan featured a bilevel base, street surfaces, and a Kettenkrad rolling through, manned by American soldiers. The movie's last scenes at the bridge made me think of a French town with a river or canal, so I wanted to include a little bit of water to evoke that image.

Building the base

I had the measurements of an actual Kettenkrad and used them to determine the size of my diorama, cutting a piece of cardboard to visualize the size. For this special diorama, I had a wooden base custom made by Al Presley of Big Al's Bases. The 9" x 9" square base is edged in finely finished walnut, **1**. I added 1" particle board as subflooring, with the higher rear level being two slabs glued together.

In the bilevel scene, I wanted the Kettenkrad on a street on the upper level. I supported the street, above a hollow space, with risers at the back edge of the board, **2**. I cut the risers from .125" styrene sheet. To account for the slight irregularity of the particle board surface, I numbered the risers so I could locate them in the same spots as where I measured them.

Photo **3** shows the base of the street surface (.125" styrene sheet) in place, on top of which I'll place a thin, vacuum-formed section of cobblestone (made by Custom Dioramics). The plastic cobblestone sheet would be wobbly without the stiff styrene underneath.

To cover the hollow space beneath the street, I faced it with sheet styrene, **4**. I had to bevel the sides so the styrene would fit against the walnut walls of the base.

5 On top of the sheet styrene I placed a vacuum-formed cobblestone street section and added a curb and sidewalk.

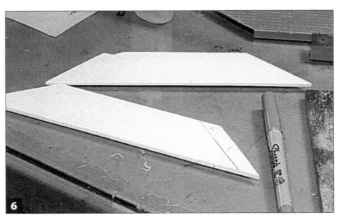

6 Another vacuum-formed piece will serve as the walkway on the lower level. Again, I needed sheet styrene to firm it up. Here, I needed a double thickness so I could elevate it above the level of the adjacent water.

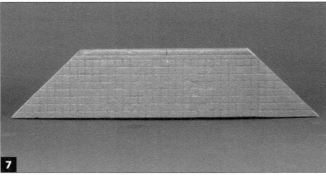

7 Then I glued the vacuum-formed walk to the two sheets of styrene.

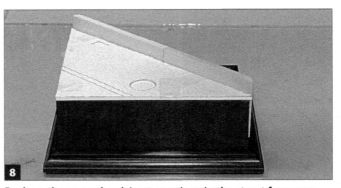

8 Back on the upper level, I cut openings in the street for a manhole cover and a storm grate. Later, I went through the sheet styrene underneath to give these openings true depth. On the long side, I raised a resin-cast retaining wall.

9 The retaining wall is comprised of two main sections of brickwork with a cap along the top. One wall section is longer than the other to avoid symmetry. The notches at the bottom ends are cut to fit the wall on the wood base.

10 I wanted to add decorative reliefs to the walls. I bought these pieces at a craft store to use as masters for molds that I could use for casting copies in resin.

The hollow space under the street can be useful. You could have a figure standing in a manhole or leave the cover askew and show some detail in the manhole opening.

Next, I cut and fit some groundwork elements before gluing them in position. I put the cobblestone street surface in place, **5**, and marked locations on it for a manhole cover and a storm grate. I added a section of vacuum-formed sidewalk behind the street.

On the lower level, the surface of the river promenade is made of more vacuum-formed plastic stonework. Like the street section above, it needed a stiff sheet-styrene backing as support. Also, since it is next to the water, it needed to be elevated. For elevation and support, I placed the vacuum-formed stonework on two laminated sheets of .125" styrene, **6**. Then I attached the walkway and curb to the sheet styrene, **7**.

Next, I glued the styrene-backed street on the upper level, **8**. In the cobblestones, I cut out the openings for the manhole cover and storm grate.

With the basic street and sidewalk portions together, I worked on the retaining wall that separates the two levels, **9**. The resin-cast wall is made up of two wall sections, three cap sections, and a decorative cameo. (The brick wall is made from parts Ben Jacobsen designed while he was

11

I already had the resin-cast brick walls on hand. To finish, I made a cap for the wall in plaster, made a mold, and then cast the cap in resin. Bouncing a motor tool with a burr bit on the plaster surface gave it the texture of a slab of concrete. The marks on the wall indicate the locations for the decorative wall reliefs.

12

Beyond the retaining wall is the street section, and then another sidewalk section.

13

Because the sidewalk is next to the water, I sealed a sheet-styrene underlayment to the base to keep resin water from seeping under the walk. At the front edge of the sidewalk, I added mounting plates for rail posts and detailed them with Grandt Line bolts.

14

In this overview of the lower level, you see, from front to back, the reservoir for the water, the waterfront sidewalk, and a retaining wall. Above the wall, you can see just a portion of the street and a wedge of curb and sidewalk at the far end.

at Kirin, a subsidiary of Dragon Models, which I always thought looked great.)

While contemplating ornamental masonry for the wall, I found some decorative doodads that I liked in a craft store, **10**. They served as masters for copies I cast from resin. I marked the locations for these pieces on the bare face of the resin wall.

I also cast the cap for the wall out of resin, **11**. I made a plaster master and, when it dried, textured it with a burr in a motor tool to give it a stony surface. After running the motor tool, I gave the plaster a light sanding to take off peaks and sharp spots left from roughing up the plaster.

I notched and sanded the bottom ends of the wall to match the edges of the wood base, **12**. I gave the left section of wall a slightly shorter run than the right to break up the symmetry.

Next, I attacked the walk by the waterfront, **13**. I placed a sheet of thick, white

styrene on the particle board under the sidewalk. This will prevent the resin I pour for water from seeping underneath the gray, vacuum-formed sidewalk, **14**. I added styrene discs and bolt heads in place on the walk as mounts for a railing. Also on the sidewalk is a MiniArt 1/35 scale park bench that I firmed it up with a strip of styrene, **15**.

To install the decorative railing (from MiniArt), I inserted brass rods in the bottoms of the poles and sank them deep into the base through the mounting plates, **16**. The rods anchor the railing and other elements. (This way, I can pull the railing from the base if I want to transport the diorama. The retaining wall, street, and sidewalk can also be pulled from the base and packed in a smaller box.)

Back on the upper level, I added some details to the street section, **17**. I glued the retainer for the manhole cover and

SMALL DETAILS

The vacuum-formed park bench, manhole cover, storm grate, sidewalk, and decorative railings are all items from MiniArt 1/35 scale set of street accessories (No. 35530). MiniArt and other manufacturers make these various everyday things that can be fabulous additions to a diorama. Instead of scratchbuilding everything, you can use these ready-made products and have more time to work on other elements that can make a diorama even better. With all the products available these days, it's easier than ever to build great dioramas.

I also have collected a huge store of spare parts, which helps when I am looking for that one specific object that I need. So be sure to keep your spare parts.

15 This gives a good view of the dimpled texture of the wall cap, which makes it look more like stone. The wall cap and resin-cast cameo relief are already primed for painting. I reinforced the MiniArt park bench with a styrene strip.

16 The railing is also a MiniArt product. I attached it to the base by placing brass rods into the poles and then inserting the poles into the mounting plates.

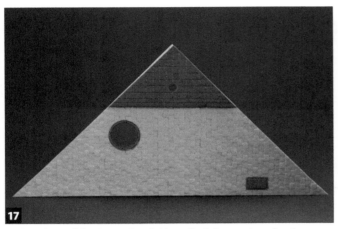

17 In this view of the upper level, I installed the retainer for the manhole cover and a storm grate in the street section (both are MiniArt items). In the sidewalk section, I cut a small hole for installing a lamppost.

18 The lamppost (another MiniArt item) is anchored by a brass tube inside styrene tubing. It sinks way into the base to help anchor everything in place.

the storm grate into the holes I had cut for them. I also cut a hole in the wedge of gray sidewalk for a mounting rod for a lamppost. The MiniArt lamppost is mounted on brass tubing inside styrene tubing, **18**. It goes deep into the base and really locks down this side of the diorama. I added the lamp shade and ornamental points to it from my spare parts, **19**. I also installed the brass cross member because the plastic part was drooping under the weight of the light fixture.

With all the elements of the base assembled and in place, I turned to the vehicles and figures, **20**. The soldiers are all from the Miniatures PMC 1/35 scale set United States Army Rangers, 2nd Ranger Battalion (No. 35005), made as passengers for a Kettenkrad. The infantry cart is made

by Bronco. It's from the DAK Fiat Topolino Italian light staff car (kit No. CB35156), and for a little cart, it sure has a lot of parts! Much of it is photoetched metal, and when you have to bend that much stuff to shape, it feels like origami!

The Kettenkrad comes from Dragon (kit. No. 6446). I added bolts that were missing from the sprocket wheel and used photoetched metal mesh in the vents. (In photo **20**, you can see one of them under the knee of the cross-legged Ranger behind the driver.) The little strips of white styrene are meant to be weld seams. I softened the styrene strips with liquid styrene cement and sculpted them with the back side of a hobby knife to make them look like welds. They're on a real Kettenkrad, so I thought they should be on my

model. I also added styrene handles.

Painting stonework

After checking the placement of the vehicles and figures, I began painting the bricks and cobblestones. My main reference for painting this stonework was *Surfaces: Visual Research for Artists, Architects, and Designers* by Judy A. Juracek (W. W. Norton). Arcane, yes, but, after all, modeling is all about the small details. This book is full of detailed photographs of different materials and construction.

For painting broad applications like this, an inexpensive, spray-can primer, Bright Touch, works as well as model-specific primers. Primer puts all the subsequent paints on an even footing, on both plastic and resin surfaces.

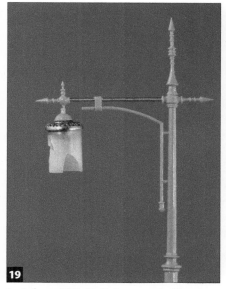

19

I reinforced MiniArt's lamppost with a brass rod to keep the light mount from drooping. I also added the decorative fixture and shade as well as the ornamental points at the top.

20

Just checking: I like to place elements as I go along to see how they work together. Adding the styrene weld seams and handles made the Kettenkrad a little more accurate. Notice how much photoetched brass is in that infantry cart behind the Kettenkrad—a tough little build!

21

Not all bricks are created equal—nor are any two exactly the same color. I used seven red and brown complementary colors that added detail and provided chromatic depth as well.

22

I dredged the paint pigments from the bottom of the tins and placed the blobs on a palette where I could pull bits of them out to mix other shades separately.

For painting bricks or cobblestone, I prefer Humbrol enamels, solvent-based paint. A lot of different colors go into creating a realistic look, **21**. I used seven complementary colors here (red, orange red, a deeper red, garage red, brown, a deeper brown, and burgundy). Then, by adding tan, black, or yellow ochre artist's oils, I easily turned those seven colors into 20 or more different shades. The artist's oils are solvent-based too, so I could mix them right in and use the same thinner as with the enamel.

While sitting in the containers, the enamel pigment settles to the bottom, and the oil, or carrier, comes to the top. I spooned out the thick pigment, which is pure color, **22**.

When using the paint in this state, it's very slow-drying. Instead of drying in 10-15 minutes, I can still get color out of pure pigment two hours later. I can work with it however I want. I can thin it with plain old cheap mineral spirits, control the drying time, and take my time applying colors.

Speaking of colors, the very first one I applied in what was a long sequence was a bright, fire engine red, **23**. I applied it in a random pattern using a flat brush, such as a No. 4, and dabbed on little splotches. I don't paint individual bricks, which I suppose you could do if you were bored, but instead produce an overlap that blends with the subsequent colors.

But before I started any blending, I applied an orange red, **24**. I don't paint straight from a pigment blob. I push a little pigment to the side and add thinner, so the paint is fairly thin.

As I added darker tones to the bricks, the paint built up and colors started to blend, **25**. After I completed the multi-hued base coat, washes continued to blend the different shades, **26**.

Sidewalks

It's the same process for the sidewalk, but with different colors. I selected seven colors complementary to gray, **27**. Again, I thinned these quite a bit, but not so much that they became transparent.

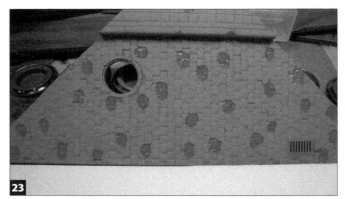

23

After applying a gray primer from a spray can and letting it dry, I started with the brightest color and dabbed it on "outside the lines."

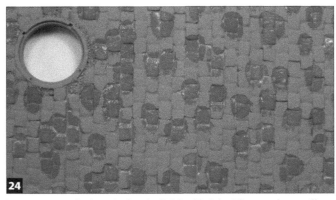

24

I was not precisely painting individual bricks. The overlaps will blend as I continue. The thinned paint appears almost translucent, but it will build up as more paint is added.

25

I used some of the darker colors here, and you can see how those blobs of pigment have contributed to other colors.

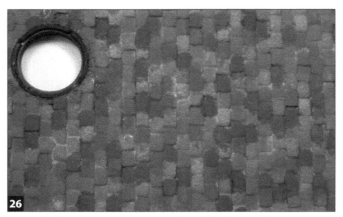

26

Once the base coat was down, washes blended and homogenized the different shades.

27

Now it's time for the sidewalks, which will be gray rather than the reddish tint of the cobblestone street. Again, I started with seven complementary colors.

28

Here, I've already applied three colors. I'm not being precise. As before, there is overlap, and those borders will fade away with the application of additional colors and washes.

I started applying the brightest colors first in very thin coats, overlapping them as I went along, **28**. After expanding my paint palette, I added some darker colors. With the base colors applied, I immediately began a series of washes, **29**.

I liberally applied the first wash of raw umber so it seeped into every little pit, crack, and line to darken those low spots, deepening them, and bringing raised details into greater relief, **30**. By applying this wash before the previous enamels were completely dry, I blended those enamels as well.

TIP: As its name implies, a wash is watery thin—1 part paint to 10 parts thinner (or even more). With this ratio, you can apply this layer after layer and gradually build up the color to the look you want.

To paint the retaining wall, I started with even more colors of paint, **31**. I used five different colors of artist's oils along with seven Humbrol enamels. In addition to the stone and brick colors, I wanted a hint of mossiness because of the wall's closeness to the water. And what an ugly bunch of colors! You would never think that turquoise and a nasty chromate green would go with those wall colors, but they did.

29 Raw umber artist's oil, here thinned with mineral spirits to a watery wash, will deepen details and further blend the various colors and shades.

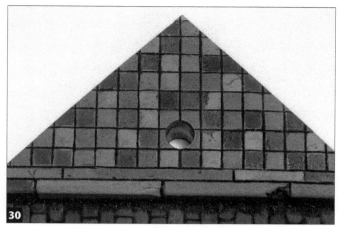

30 The wash settled in recesses and low spots, making raised details more prominent and showing off engraved details in the molding. If the wash pools up, you can use a cotton swab or a rag and soak up excess.

31 Next up is the vertical retaining wall. Because of its proximity to water, that side of the wall should be mossy in spots. So, in addition to my seven basic enamels, I added in more artist's oils.

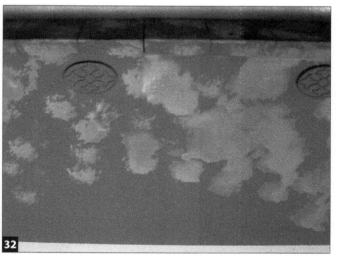

32 On the street side of the wall, stippling with a beat-up brush produced a marbled texture…

I painted the bricks in the wall facing the water as I had done for the previous stonework, and started here with khaki. On the street side of the wall, I turned its smooth surface into a marbled one by stippling the colors, **32**. Marble is not just one color; it has veins and grain and different shades of green and blue in a naturally random array. Nothing pretty, just random jabs at the wall with a loaded brush. (You don't want a good brush for stippling; in this instance, rougher is better.)

Back on the water side, I continued to add color to the bricks, including a garish green that, believe it or not, eventually faded into the other colors, **33**.

I wanted to give the cameo on the wall a weathered patina, **34**. This piece wears more artist's oils than enamels; I wanted it to dry more slowly to give me time to work. I started with some blues, tans, and an overcoat of some pretty ugly turquoise green.

While the cameo was still wet, I added different shades of turquoise and tan, and some random streaks of white artist's oil (with a little Naples yellow added) to emphasize a rain-streaked look, and a weathered patina began to emerge. A few downward strokes of a brush blended the colors and produced those streaks.

TIP: I use cheap thinner, just mineral spirits, in my washes. If you use the manufacturer's thinner, the paint will dry more quickly—but it also breaks the pigments down more, and you get little suspended bits. Mixing washes takes some experimentation. Using mineral spirits is OK for Humbrol enamels and Winsor & Newton artist's oils, but there are paints it could mess up. If you're going to use other brands, test for results.

Once the base coats were completed, the colors still looked a little wild, but the next steps blended the colors, and then I finished by selectively redefining sharp details that faded in the blending process.

The difference was a series of washes. A raw umber wash emphasized the brick lines and began to blend some of those

33

…while on the water side, mossy tones appeared.

34

I had some special painting in mind for this cameo relief, which I imagined would be cast in metal. I wanted a weathered patina. At left is the turquoise base coat. At right, I applied white artist's oil (mixed with Naples yellow) to the high spots and, with a dry brush, dragged it down to replicate rain streaking.

35

Dark washes blended all these crazy colors and shades and helped define textures.

36

I applied several layers of a dark wash, building it up gradually rather than trying to get this look all in one coat. I also applied the wash to the cameo in order to raise its finish.

37

On the left, you can see how the wash faded and blended colors. On the right side, I treated the grout with a pinwash (thicker than a wash) to sharpen the lines between the bricks.

38

Here, you can see that the bricks are more defined, their colors varied but now unified by washes. The variety of colors and shades is more realistic than a brick wall painted one color.

weird colors, **35**. I didn't apply this wash to the cameo.

I applied a second wash, raw umber darkened with olive drab, **36**. This time I treated the cameo because the wash would raise the finish on the cameo, and that's what I wanted. I wanted it to look a little crusty.

Photo **37** illustrates what washes can accomplish. A large patch left of the cameo shows the faded, blended look of

the two washes. To restore some definition to the bricks, I outlined them with a thin, dark umber artist's acrylic pinwash (so named by armor modelers who use a pin or a very fine brush to pick out individual bolts, latches, and other small parts). For the pinwash, I used artist's acrylics made by Golden and some Holbein artist's acrylics. The acrylics lay on top of the enamel beneath them, rather than seep into the enamels.

These precisely placed colors made the bricks more defined and unified the varied colors, **38**. On the cameo, I selectively detailed the recessed features of the casting to bring the high spots into greater relief.

After another look, I wasn't satisfied with how the stonework looked. But when I gave it a watery wash of Winsor & Newton blue black artist's oil (about 1 part paint to 10 parts thinner), it looked much

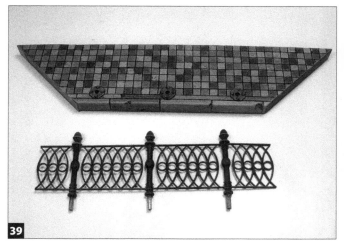

39

The lower sidewalk and waterfront railing were ready for assembly. Aluminum rod in the base of the rail posts fit the mounts installed in the sidewalk.

40

I experimented with different types of water. The square chunk at bottom right is pure resin, which became rock hard. At bottom left is Magic Water, an acrylic mix, with blue added to it. At the top is Castin' Craft clear polyester resin with Humbrol green and brown enamels, which is the one used.

41

I sealed the reservoir for the resin water to prevent seepage under the sidewalk. The reservoir is base-coated with flat black and ready for pouring. Base-coating the edges of the base with flat black prevents bright spots of unpainted plastic or wood from showing in any gaps between the base's components.

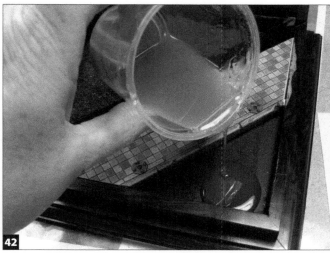

42

After gently mixing green and brown acrylics into the resin for a riverine color, I poured the resin slowly to avoid introducing bubbles.

better. It made the pinwash look a little less stark and muted the brightest colors.

While the stonework dried, I built and painted the railings and other elements to go on the base, **39**. It might be hard to see, but the railing has all sorts of colors in it, including reds and greens.

Changing resin into water

There are several different ways to model water, and the skills required vary with the body of water. Different modeling methods and techniques can depict ocean waves, mountain streams, or a still pond.

I experimented with a few different products before deciding on the materials and the look I wanted for what I imagined was a canal next to my street and walkway, **40**. I wanted to learn about these products and see how they were to work with: how long it would be before I could touch it, how could I clean the top, those sort of things. I wanted to know about curing time, durability, and rigidity. That way, if I had to do the process more than once, I would know how it would turn out each time.

Magic Water is an acrylic substance. I

added green and blue artist's oils to it, and it stayed rubbery and, despite the different paints, just stayed blue. I also tried a polyester resin, and that got as hard as Bakelite—what telephones were made of in the days when the receiver could be used as a weapon. I didn't like the look of it.

Castin' Craft clear polyester resin turned out to be the winner. I tinted it with Humbrol green and brown enamels. When that shrank as it cured, I added a clear layer of Envirotex two-part polyurethane, which added an illusion of depth to the water.

43

44

The result is the placid water of a river or canal. After pouring the resin, I laid a sheet of paper over, but not touching it, to keep dust off while the resin dried and cured. Once you've poured this resin and it is curing, you have to be patient. It takes three or four days before you can do anything with it. However you cover it, make sure to allow for ventilation.

While the resin dried, I got after the GIs and the Kettenkrad. I adjusted the fit of the figures to the vehicle while I assembled them. Then I dug through my spares box for various packs to stow on the vehicles.

45

46

It's 1944, so I gave the Kettenkrad the late-war German three-color camouflage scheme. I left the packs stowed and painted them individually as I went along. The first coat was Tamiya dark yellow (XF-60). Then I airbrushed a thin layer of a lightened shade of the same dark yellow for highlights.

Next, I airbrushed a freehand pattern of Tamiya red brown (XF-64) followed by Tamiya dark green (XF-81). This matched the camouflage on the Kettenkrad in *Saving Private Ryan*.

While my water samples were curing, I painted the interior of the base to ensure that no bare, bright wood or styrene would show through anywhere along the joints of the base assembly, **41**.

The directions for Castin' Craft called for 15 drops of catalyst per ounce of resin. I like to measure any two-part liquid solution, whether it's casting resin or polyester resin water, using an accurate electronic scale. That way I can be absolutely sure of the proportions for any mix and repeat them if needed. The best ratio for the water was 1:10 catalyst to resin.

I gently mixed in the Humbrol green and brown enamel, and slowly poured the resin to avoid introducing air bubbles, **42**. This stuff stinks to high heaven! Make

sure you have ample ventilation when you working with it.

After the resin was poured, I laid a sheet of paper over it to keep dust off. Absolutely do not touch it! Regardless of the package directions, I recommend that you leave it completely alone for at least 72 hours, **43**. Once it's cured, you can clean it with a lens cloth, computer wipe, or can of compressed air. If you're going to display a diorama for any amount of time, you have to keep dust off it.

Get on the rabbit

I loaded up the Kettenkrad with stowage out of my scrap box and assembled and test-fit the figures, **44**. Then I was ready to paint.

I base-coated the Kettenkrad with Tamiya dark yellow, **45**. Then I added highlights, using a mixture of the base coat plus flesh and white. Next, came camouflage streaks to represent the late-war German three-color scheme, **46**. I used German red brown and German dark green for the streaks, putting the red brown on first.

With the Kettenkrad painted, the figures were ready for a test-ride on the street, **47**. On the vehicle's headlight, I added a self-adhesive sequin as a headlight lens. (This craft-store item is called Shimmering Dots.) On the sidewalk, the lamppost was in place, painted with a gloss dark green but waiting for weathering. I still had a few other details to finish and the figures to paint.

Putting on uniforms and moving out

After finishing the vehicles and ground-work, I was finally ready to paint the stars of the show—the figures. I painted the faces with artist's oils. (See chapter 4 for more on how to paint figures.)

For the soldiers' fatigues, I basically used two colors of acrylic paints and varied their shades, **48**. Certain equipment, such as helmets, could be closer to the same color, but different types of fabric on different people calls for variety. I started painting part of a figure's uniform with one color, mixed a different shade of that color, and then painted a different part of the next figure's uniform with that color, and so on. I changed shades as I went along to provide credible variety in making the figures look individual.

American colors are an extra challenge as there are so many—olive, khaki, field drabs—and it's hard to find them pre-mixed. I hand-mixed every color I used for these American uniforms.

After applying the base coats, I used a lighter shade of each base coat for highlights, **49**. For the first round of highlights, I added a little flesh to the base.

Then I added a little more flesh and a little white to superhighlight. Following that step, I added a little more white to the mix to catch just the high spots. Then, I dialed that back and added dark green and black to the base. I selectively applied

Shimmering Dots, a product found in craft stores, adds realistic shine to the headlight as a lens. As you can see, I still had plenty to paint.

I used two different olive drabs as well as mixed shades. The trousers of the two figures at each end and the jacket of the driver (second from right) are close in color—but not quite the same. Varying the shades of uniforms individualizes the figures.

49

After a base coat, I lightened the base color and dry-brushed it to highlight details. Then I lightened it a little more and used a gentle dry-brushing for superhighlights, such as on the helmet.

50

Most of the figures' uniforms were painted with various shades of the two colors you see here. Flowing a darker shade into folds and wrinkles brought out the details.

51

It was almost time to get on the rabbit. I had edges to clean up, a lamppost and riverside railing to weather some more, but otherwise the scene was nearly complete.

these darker shades to the wrinkles and folds in the uniforms, **50**.

On the weapons, I first painted the rifle stocks flesh. I then overcoated them with an artist's oil—burnt umber or burnt sienna—and let them sit for about 20 minutes. Then I dipped a short-bristled brush in thinner and used it to streak the oil paints until the flesh color started showing through and it looked like wood grain. I sealed it with a thin layer of acrylic semigloss.

I used the same principle of varying olive drab for the knapsacks stowed on the Kettenkrad, **51**. There were still details to attend to—finishing edges, weathering the lamppost and railings, and perhaps another wash or round or two of dry-brushing. But it was almost there, and soon these GIs would be ready to roll through France, cross the Rhine, and take Berlin.

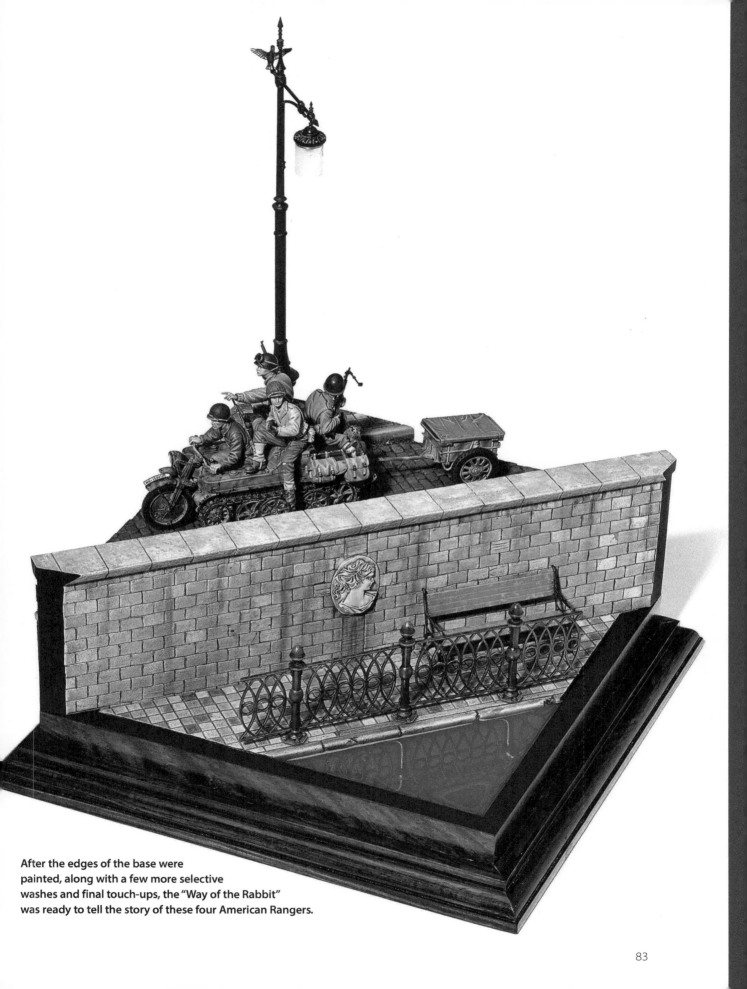

After the edges of the base were
painted, along with a few more selective
washes and final touch-ups, the "Way of the Rabbit"
was ready to tell the story of these four American Rangers.

8

Defenders of the Reich

In the last days of World War II, what's left of Germany's best soldiers mounts a desperate defense in a losing cause. There is a lot of action and angst packed into this compact vignette.

The design and conception of this piece dates back to my days with Warriors Models, the company John Rosengrant and I created. One day, our sculptor, Tony Williams, described the scene for this diorama, and I did a quick sketch—it looked like something you would draw on an Etch-A-Sketch. Then, he sculpted the figures to fit my crudely drawn base.

1 Having imagined the composition and made some rough sketches, I used big slabs of styrene plastic foam to build a substrata that I covered with Apoxie Sculpt, real dirt, and general debris. Each brick is an individual casting, and I built the wall one brick at a time, like a mason.

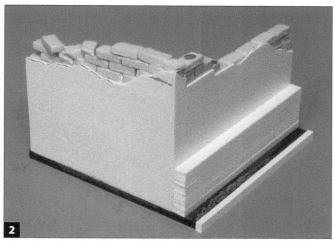

2 The outer, vertical sheets of styrene will become stucco. The steps on the right will come in handy later in posing a soldier who is scaling that wall.

3 Using earth-colored Apoxie Sculpt for landscaping saved on the amount of paint and real dirt I used to cover it with. I mixed in more bricks, some kitty litter, and odd shards of styrene for other debris.

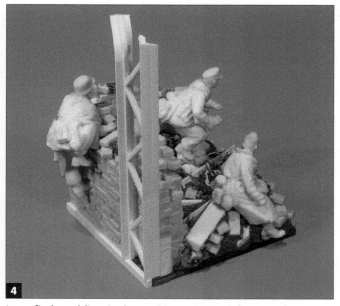

4 I test-fit the soldiers in the positions I wanted them, so they looked like they were in the rubble, not on the rubble.

I did two versions of the vignette, a Wehrmacht version and an SS version. I completed the Wehrmacht version for Warriors and sold it as a commission piece. But I liked the scene so much that I wanted to do another one.

The Wehrmacht version

Although the vignettes differed substantially in composition, the bases were built essentially the same way, with stepped sheets of styrene providing relief underneath the groundwork to come, **1**. Using plastic foam or styrene saves on the amount of Apoxie Sculpt or Celluclay you might need to build up an earthen base.

All of the bricks were mine: I made 10 different masters, molded the bricks, and cast them in resin. And just as you would build a real wall, I laid each of those individual bricks in the vignette's walls. I also glued a few bricks on the "floor" to hold the groundwork putty in place. Sometimes, with a very smooth surface, when

the putty dries, it actually pops off as one piece, and you don't want that.

Then, I drilled through the bricks into the base and inserted brass rod, which I bent over at the top for more anchoring power. The sheet styrene on the exterior of the bricks serves as a wall treatment such as stucco, **2**. In one spot on the exterior wall, I added a step, which was later covered with bricks.

I built up the groundwork with earthtoned Apoxie Sculpt (it comes in different

5

Those steps on the back wall are now mostly covered with bricks, but I left a few out so the soldier can climb the wall.

6

I brush-painted the bricks, but not all the same color. I painted a few with one color…

7

…then mixed 15-20 more hues because all the bricks were not the same color. Mixing artist's oils with Humbrol enamels gave me a virtually infinite choice of colors, hues, and shades.

colors) and covered it with finely sifted real dirt, kitty litter, and broken bricks, **3**. I also added pieces of solder to represent pipes and conduits from the ruined building and I-beams made of styrene.

As I built up the groundwork with the Apoxie Sculpt, I test-fit the figures, **4**. I wanted them to look as if they were standing in—and not on—the rubble. While the putty was still wet and workable, I put Vaseline on the figures at the points where they would contact the base. I pushed them into the brickwork and putty and let them set overnight. The next day, I snapped the figures out, and they left nice, tight indentations where they fit into the base.

Speaking of in, and not on, the figure on the back wall got his toeholds on the steps I created earlier, where I strategically omitted a few bricks for the soldier's feet, **5**.

When I was satisfied with the groundwork, rubble, and the soldiers' positions, I primed everything with Floquil gray primer, let it dry, and then began painting the walls, **6**. I created a large palette of colors for the bricks, **7**. Using Humbrol enamels, I picked out seven or eight colors ranging from tan to a deep reddish purple. Then I added some artist's oils to the enamels and expanded the colors to about 20 different shades.

By using all those different colors, none of the bricks looked quite the same.

In Europe, this building was probably a couple of hundred years old. During that time, weathering would have affected the coloring, and a number of them would have been replaced, which also would have produced different coloring. Because of this, I wanted a wide variation in colors, and when finished, the detailed look multiplied the Wow Factor, **8**.

SS version

After completing the Wermacht diorama, I varied the design of the SS version. I wanted this one to be fuller and more compact, with all the action flowing outward, **9**. I tightened up the space. The base became a little taller and a little more vertical, but, overall, it was not as big as the first one.

I composed the scene, cast the bricks, and built the walls, which were actually constructed of two layers of bricks. Laying the bricks one at a time took a while! In places, I left portions of the inner wall crumbling. It may look random, but I planned it that way according to how the figures would fit.

The composition of a scene is your vision, but when you go to fit the figures,

This is the first "Defenders of the Reich," which I call the *Wehrmacht version*. I liked it well enough to want to try another version to see if I could improve on it—and because I sold this one!

FINDING MOTIVATION

Soon after completing the Wehrmacht diorama, I started the SS version, but then it sat on the shelf for about two years. One day, Mig Jimenez, of AK Interactive, came to my house for a visit. While he sat on the floor wrestling with my two dogs, he noticed the uncompleted SS version and said, "That's a very nice vignette. You ought to finish it." That comment from a friend was all it took for me to get going. It was already built and primed, so I pulled it off the shelf and had it finished within a week.

you might have to make changes. That's why I continually check the figures' fit.

As I painted, I stopped every now and then to test-fit the figures because sometimes even an infinitesimal bit of paint alters that nice, tight fit, **10**. If it does, then I go back and scrape off a little bit of paint so the figure fits its "sockets" in the base.

In the SS version of the diorama, the scene is more vertical, with a tighter composition, and more action taking place in a slightly smaller space. The base has been primed.

10

I test-fit the figures often because they had to fit tightly into, not on top of, this rubble. Believe it or not, even a little paint can hinder the fit.

11

Like the first diorama, this one has a figure scaling the wall in back. I built a special notch into the bricks to give him a foothold. You can also see how rough the bricks look after years of damage and weathering.

12

Washes and dry-brushing diversify the rubble and make features more distinct.

13

Using a fine brush, I painted mortar between the bricks. It's like tuckpointing with paint!

14

Notice the double layer of bricks. At this point, every little detail is designed around the figures. The long, wood box at the left is an ammunition box, but I was not through painting it yet.

Speaking of fitting, the soldier at the back is on his brick-covered step, **11**. This photo gives you a good look at the hand-laid brick wall and how rough some of the bricks are. In an old building, after hundreds of years of settling, along with wartime damage, bricks will become mis-aligned or work themselves loose.

After putting the initial coat of paint on the bricks, I began weathering the walls and rubble with a series of washes and dry-brushing, **12**. I started with an overall wash of raw umber. Immediately after applying the wash, I took the masking off the base to make sure none of the wash seeped under the tape. If any had, I wiped

it off immediately with a soft tissue, so it didn't ruin the finish on the wood.

I kept the wood part of the base clean through the painting process to prevent buildup of adhesive residue from the tape or thinners from etching the wood finish.

After the wash dried, I used a fine brush to paint mortar between the bricks, **13**.

15

I gave the ammo box a wood layer and then painted it dark green. I removed some of the green with alcohol, so the color underneath showed through to make the box look battle-worn.

16

In more detail painting, I added a chalk construction marking on the girder above the wall, which was exposed when the wall fell (or was blown) down.

17

I added a swastika to the wall as the first element of the graffiti I planned for the wall.

18

What you see here is not the wall, but an image of the wall. I scanned the wall into my computer, placed the white lettering in the image, and printed it out. Backing it with masking tape (purple) stiffened it a little to make it easier to cut out the letters and make a stencil.

I painted the girders with four different layers of paint: base coat, shadow, highlight, and superhighlight. The base was Floquil gray primer, which has a relatively rough finish that provided great "tooth" for the following coats. To add shadows, I used black, followed by artist's oil washes of burnt umber. Then, to highlight, I used yellow ochre and burnt sienna oils. I also highlighted the emerald green light hanging from the girder with a lighter shade of green.

TIP: Oils are the most versatile paint you can use. If you apply them in translucent layers, as I do, they will dry fairly quickly, unlike an opaque layer of oils that you might use to paint figures or a picture. Those can take days to dry. But if the oils are very thin, such as in a wash, they soak into that Floquil primer and wham! They dry quickly.

While the final layers were still wet, I lined the edges with yellow ochre. Then I took a brush with a little thinner to feather it in, softening the color edge so it was not a line but simply a highlight.

Then I turned my attention to some of the smaller details, such as the long wood box that holds ammunition for the Panzerschreck, a German antitank weapon. To paint the wood ammo box, I first applied a layer of flesh acrylic. When that dried, I overcoated it with a burnt sienna artist's oil. I let that coat dry for about 10 minutes, then streaked it with a brush to pull off a little of the burnt sienna, which revealed the flesh color underneath and produced a faux wood grain, **14**.

The next layer I applied to the ammo box was a German feldgrau (dark green), which left worn spots on the edges, **15**. You think about how the real box was built and painted, and how it was used. It would have been dragged around, and by the time it wound up in this scene, it would look pretty beat up.

There is other detail painting visible in this same shot. Note the orange, yellow, and red highlights on the bricks. And on the lower right, there's a slab of concrete with cracks painted on it.

I painted on more of those tiny details that add realism and get your attention, **16**. On one of the top beams, there are markings on it that haven't been seen

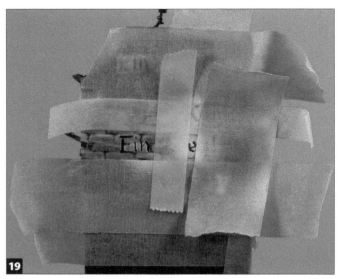

19 Here, the wall was covered by the stencil. Being extra careful not to damage the paint with adhesive, I airbrushed one letter at a time rather than burnishing the whole stencil at once.

20 "A Fight, A Victory!" was now painted on the wall. But I'll have to touch up the overspray and make it look less freshly painted.

21 That's more like it! A combination of brush-painting and a little sanding here and there knocked the newness off.

22 There's that ammo box again. I brush-painted the lettering on the box, but it was so tiny that I didn't paint real lettering—it only looked that way.

since the structure was erected. Note the European-style numeral 1.

The swastika was the first element of some graffiti that I applied to that wall, based on a wartime photo I saw, **17**. The lettering is in a font called Alpine, which has a German look to it, **18**. I actually scanned the wall, placed the lettering in the image on my computer, sized it to the same scale as the model (measured in millimeters), and printed it out with the lettering in place. I attached low-tack tape to the back of the printed image to stiffen the paper a little, and cut out the lettering with a hobby knife to make a stencil.

Because I was worried about damaging the paint on the wall, I used very little adhesive to attach the stencil to the wall. I airbrushed Tamiya white, one letter at a time, covering the nearest letters with low-tack tape that I gently burnished onto the wall through the open letters to minimize overspray, **19**. What little overspray there was around some of the letters I easily touched up by adding some more weathering and colors to the bricks, **20**.

Bright, freshly painted graffiti wouldn't look right in this situation, so I toned it down with artist's oil washes of raw umber, burnt sienna, and Van Dyke brown,

and, in certain spots, by just scraping the white paint off the wall, **21**.

While I had the white paint and brush out, I brush-painted a stenciled legend on the ammo box, **22**—another one of those tiny, minute details that people like to look at and enjoy. For a detail that small, I used a form of pointalism. The letters don't have to be legible at that size, so I painted tiny dots along the lines of lettering, and then connected the dots with a little more white paint, all applied with a very fine brush.

I kept looking at the brick wall and applied more shadow, **23**. Around the corner from the graffiti I deepened the

23 At right, you can see how dark washes, followed by dry-brushing in a lighter shade, made the stones and pebbles on the bricks stand out.

24 Here you can see more dry-brushing of debris and the ends of the bricks. I also test-fit the soldiers again before their final placement.

25 More detail painting. Like the ammo box, the Panzerschreck (anti-tank weapon) needed to look chipped and worn. After applying a dark yellow base coat I brush-painted the scratches and such with black green.

26 Speaking of details, it's late winter in Germany as the war winds down—and that requires a wet and crusty-looking snow. I used microballoons, tiny beads of glass, to give the snow its sparkle. And with that, the second version of the diorama was complete.

recessed areas and dry-brushed the rubble with some brighter colors to make it pop. I also brush-painted more mortar to further vary the colors.

Then it was time for another test-fitting, **24**. In this photo, you can see more dry-brushing.

And I still was not through painting little details, **25**. On the Panzerschreck, the base coat was dark yellow, the same as many German armored vehicles. I brushed on "chipped" paint, very thin black green, and flowed lighter shades along the edges of the chips to add dimension.

The diorama was just about done, but I thought it still needed something—snow! Thinking about the location and the way the soldiers are dressed, it only made sense that there should be some of the white stuff around, **26**. The snow was a combination of ingredients: Liquitex acrylic gloss medium for the wet-looking base, to which I added a mixture of Snow Coat (scale snow from the The Small Shop EU), and microballoons. I applied the Liquitex, sprinkled on the Snow Coat and microballoons, and blew off the excess.

TIP: Microballoons look great for snow, and give it the right sparkle, but it is really wicked stuff—microballoons are tiny, and they're glass. Always use eye protection and a two-canister, OSHA-rated respirator. You do not want to inhale or ingest it!

The addition of snow helped fix the time of the story told by "Defenders of the Reich," which would have been January or February 1945. Surrender would come in May, but, for Germany, the writing was already on the wall—and unlike the weathered graffiti on these bricks, it didn't say victory.

9

Iranian Pasdaran patrol

Somewhere in the Iranian desert, an M38A1C plys the sands as the Iranian Pasdaran (Revolutionary Guard) rides the pipelines of the National Iranian Oil Co. The vehicle is a 1/35 scale Skybow kit (No. TP3505, now AFV Club kit No. AF35S19).

In World War II, American jeeps were built by Willys-Overland and Ford. But after the war, Willys-Overland won naming rights and continued to make them, eventually producing a civilian version (CJ) that would serve as a developmental base for its improved military jeep, the M38A1.

After the Korean War, these jeeps were produced for export. With more than 45,000 made and sold around the world, they could be found in military forces almost everywhere—and their reputation for durability continued to prove itself as many of the vehicles, now more than 50 years old, still show up in contemporary images.

1 Before painting the model, test-fit the figures, preferably in a second test vehicle. After placing the figures, check to see if you have to move any equipment so there are no conflicts.

2 I adapt the kit parts, cast in olive, to fit a turned-metal barrel from Eduard to build up a 106mm recoilless rifle.

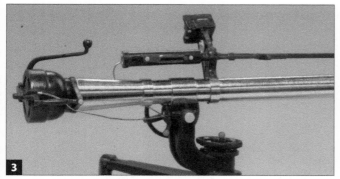

3 Bits of styrene stock and snippets of .5-amp lead fuse wire add detail. The red knobs are tiny beads from a craft store. You can find materials anywhere. You just have to use your imagination.

4 Modeling wear and tear starts early in the process. Here, I roughed up a rear quarter-panel with a motor tool.

5 I let the motor tool have its way, skipping and skidding across surfaces to produce scrapes and dents. I follow it with Tamiya liquid cement and steel wool to take the fuzz off the surfaces.

6 Up front, the motor tool plays havoc with the fenders, bumper, and grille. I use brass wire for the M38A1C's distinctive headlight guards.

7 Brass wire also serves as grab handles on the hood. It's finer than the kit parts but more realistic than the photoetched metal found in many detail kits, which looks too two-dimensional.

8 In the back, I cut tie-down bands from .005" lead sheet and add pieces of styrene for cinches. Lead sheet is available from MMD and other sources, including wine bottles.

9 Installing the gun assembly arms the jeep. I add more tie-downs in back and craft beads on the gear shifts. These simple details add up to a more complex, detailed look.

10 Along the way, I continue to pose the figures with the equipment. That's my resin-cast gas can holder on the starboard side of the jeep, and additional shells in the aft stowage. (I dug into my spares box for these pieces.) This shows the last steps before painting.

11 I remove the stowed equipment and gun to apply a base coat: Gunze Sangyo Aqueous Hobby Color H70, RLM 02—a World War II color commonly found in bay interiors of German aircraft.

12 Next, I lighten the base color with Tamiya acrylic flat flesh (XF-15), misting it on for a highlight coat that lets the darker base remain in shadows and recessed lines.

13 Shading highlights and the darker base color emphasize recesses and details by bringing them into sharper contrast and greater relief. I'll airbrush a darker shade of the base color in wheel wells and under overhangs to imply shadows.

14 A very dilute wash of black (95 percent thinner) tones the color down. Pinwashes of burnt sienna and raw umber artist's oils settle into details, toning down highlights and deepening surface features. The tires are detailed with valve stems made from brass rod.

I built a recoilless rifle variant, M38A1C, and assigned it to the Pasdaran, Iran's Revolutionary Guard. The project was inspired by my friend Charlie Pritchett, who lived in Iran during his childhood when his father worked there.

Regarding composition, I try to keep things simple, while also trying to put as much into that confined space as I can. As

this diorama took shape, the focal point remained dead center on the base. Your eyes take you right to the center: the hood of the jeep and the barrel of the recoilless rifle. Within the perimeter, you've got decals on the pipeline, two figures, the headlights of the jeep, the jeep's hood, and the groundwork. The gun determines a lot of the focus. Your eyes are drawn to

that barrel, which is centered with the centered mass of the pipelines. This is a pivotal concept, and if you alter it, for instance, positioning the jeep in the opposite direction, it doesn't work the same.

Most of this chapter is about detailing and finishing the jeep. (Chapter 2 contains information about adding groundwork to the base.)

15 You can use pinwashes for stains such as fuel spillage around the gas tank. I like Winsor & Newton Indian red and burnt sienna oils for brighter touches.

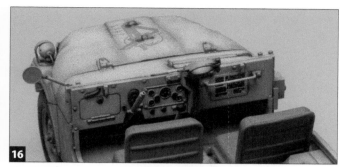

16 I brush-paint the instrument dials and use the kit decals for the vehicle information placards on the passenger side.

17 Bits of dark color applied with a fine brush represent chipped paint. I was careful to keep it looking random and unaffected. Here, a little goes a long way. If it looks like you did it, it's too much.

18 Wear and tear mounts up on the front end of the jeep, Although I used MV Products lenses for these headlights, since then I've discovered adhesive-backed EKSuccess Stickos, which are found in craft stores with the scrapbooking supplies.

19 Charlie Pritchett designed this decal. It's an emblem of the Pasdaran (ideological arm of the Revolutionary Guard). Multiple applications of decal solution and Pledge Future make the decal conform and look like it was painted on.

20 I airbrush the gun with Tamiya flat black (XF-1), then add washes of blue black oil, Tamiya clear blue (X-23), and smoke (X-19). I highlight raised edges with Berol Prismacolor aluminum pencil. Dark oils replicate dirt around the gunlock and windshield.

The jeep is manned by Warriors' 1/35 scale Iranian M38 jeep crew. In posing the figures, it's important that they look natural, so you need to decide if it is necessary to alter any of their poses. To determine the best fit, I built a second jeep to use as a test vehicle to avoid any damage to the diorama's model and test-fit the soldiers in it.

Painting and weathering

I paint the vehicle with a dark base coat for preshading, then lighter coats for highlights with selective shadowing, and follow that with washes to homogenize these coats. Recently, this process of replicating the effects of light on an object has been called *color modulation*, but I first encountered it as *highlights and shadows*,

as it was called by Verlinden.

The key to the weathered finish is a series of several washes. I use artist's oils and cheap, cheap paint thinner for very thin washes—I mean really thin, about 95 per-cent paint thinner, in several applications.

Then I use pinwashing, a selective application of dark washes to specific details. I use a "wet-on-wet" process,

21 I take similar steps, and a lot of time, with finishing the shell canisters and straps. I apply the metallic pencil to hard edges and other spots where getting knocked around produces bare metal. This treatment at once defines shape and realistically represents rugged service.

22 After several layers of detailing, painting, shading, weathering, chipping, and highlighting, my M38A1C, with its 106mm recoilless rifle serves as the centerpiece of my pipeline diorama.

keeping the area wet with thinner so when I put the paintbrush down, I don't get capillary action that spreads paint all over the place. It'll stay exactly where I want it to because it's already wet underneath. And by keeping it wet, you can actually take a brush and run streaks out for different effects. If you don't like the

effect, you can just remove it with more thinner on a cloth or brush.

To model paint chipping, I prefer using Golden Artist acrylics: burnt umber, sepia, and black. These paints come highly diluted.

Here, the black, being so thin, takes on some of the tan coming through after I put it down, and it gave some relief, look-

ing like it's been chipped. You see some of the tan coming through, but it actually works the opposite way to give it that relief, like it has a lip on it. It's the opposite from the theory of how it really should be—the dark showing underneath the desert tan where the paint has chipped—but visually it works.

The main piece in this diorama, set in Mogadishu during the 1990s, is a Mig Productions resin Toyota Land Cruiser BJ45, 1/35 scale, kit No. 35208, with a Soviet B11 recoilless rifle (107mm).

Warfare in the Third World is often a low-budget operation in which modern weapons and fighting vehicles are in short supply. In such asymmetrical conflicts, where warring factions consist of irregular fighting forces, irregular equipment is *de rigueur*.

To enhance the model, I added some of my own details, especially to the weapons. I fit the kit's recoilless rifle with an aftermarket 106mm barrel. The .30-caliber machine gun is a resin casting; I detailed a plastic weapon and used it as a master for a mold. The shells and casings in the back of the jeep are also my castings. The jerry can rack is a Verlinden Productions resin piece with straps cut from thin lead sheet. Hinges for the doors were shaped from sheet styrene. I used brass rod and craft beads for the width indicators. I robbed the hood latches from another kit.

To begin the heavy weathering, I took my trusty motor tool to the front bumper. (It's a Foredom, the kind that jewelers and dentists use, with a foot control and geared to go slow, unlike others that can just tear things up.) To bend the bumper that severely, I used a hairdryer to soften the resin. But I couldn't mess it up to the point where I couldn't attach it to the front end; the locators had to stay close enough for me to attach the part. So I made a mockup mount, took the hairdryer to the bumper, and bent it up. After letting it cool, I popped it off the mockup mount and glued it to the Land Cruiser. I made the tie rods from styrene rod and valve stems for the tires from brass wire.

I added tread plate for the running board (a photoetched-metal part from On the Mark). The license-plate mount is sheet styrene. I detailed the machine-gun mount using styrene rod with lead mounting strips and bolts from my Waldron punch-and-die set.

Here's a closer look at the machine-gun mount and the door hinges I made. I used brass rod on the mount for the recoilless rifle.

STORY BEHIND A KIT

The Mig Productions 1/35 scale kit of the Toyota Land Cruiser was actually modeled after a 1/24 scale Esci kit that came from my collection. It was a high-dollar kit, very rare and expensive. My buddy Charlie Pritchett took it with him to Spain when he visited Mig Jimenez. Mig fell in love with it and wanted to produce a kit of it in 1/35 scale.

Fighters have been devising ways to make weapons mobile since shortly after the invention of the wheel. During World War II, British and Commonwealth jeeps and Land Rovers rigged with machine guns fought in the North African desert. In the 1980s, the war between Chad and Libya was sometimes called "The Toyota War" for the number of armed Toyota HiLux pickup trucks used by both sides.

During the 1990s, in Somalia, unarmed United Nations and nongovernment organizations in Mogadishu found it prudent to hire local guards and drivers for protection,

paying for them with "technical assistance grants." Eventually, the vehicles secured by these grants became known as *technicals*.

My variation on this theme is a Toyota Land Cruiser armed with a Russian 107mm recoilless rifle. The vehicle is one that would be found with Mohamed Farrah Aidid's clan, the Habr Gidr.

The scene is set in Mogadishu. The composition is keyed by battle damage, rubble, and heavily distressed and degraded paint—weathering to the extreme. (Chapter 2 describes how I built the groundwork for this diorama.)

5

In the back, you can see the same canisters that I used on the M38A1C Iranian jeep in chapter 9, as they came from the same castings. The real tubes are made of pressed cardboard. I bored out the castings to make them look like empty cylinders. I also resin-cast the ammunition inside the tube. The really thin metal strips are .002" lead foil.

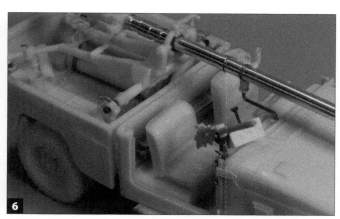

6

You can see some of the details I added to the gun. It is extremely hard to glue resin to aluminum, so I "pickled" the barrel first: I took steel wool to it and soaked it in apple vinegar for about 15 minutes. This etched the metal and made it more receptive to super glue. To apply the glue on the mounting straps, I put a little super glue on a No. 11 blade and ran it along the edges. If you try to position it and apply glue directly, it's hard to maneuver. So I put the part in place and tacked it down with a little super glue.

7

The homemade gunlock, resin gunsight, and maneuvering handles were a pain to glue on. Up front, there's a headlight plug hanging out, which I made from brass wire and resin carved to shape. A vehicle like this ought to have a smashed headlight.

8

Next, I began the painting process. The base coat was a glossy, custom mix of Tamiya acrylics that was an exact match for the Toyota color, using green (X-5), flat black (X-1), a little orange (X-6), and some light green (X-15). When airbrushing a resin piece like this, it's hard to cover. I had to put on two layers.

9

I highlighted the paint to replicate light play and bring out details. I added Tamiya desert yellow (XF-59) and orange to the base coat and hit the high spots. The edges still were darker green.

10

Here you can see the outlining effect of a highlight coat. You can see the darker green at the edges of the hood and fender.

11 Mother Nature plays hell with any vehicle that stays out in the sun. To replicate sunbleaching, I first taped off the hood and highlighted the inner panels by airbrushing those spots with Alclad II bright aluminum (even though Land Cruisers are made of steel, not aluminum). I panel-faded it to make the paint look uneven. I covered the rest of the model during this painting session because the Alclad atomized so finely, and I didn't want to wind up with sparkles all over the vehicle.

12 This layer began with a coat of Pledge Future floor polish to protect the metallic paint. Then, I gave it a coat of Testors Dull-cote and brush-painted rust with Vallejo dark brown acrylics. I took time to highlight the inner areas of oxidization with tiny, bright touches of metallics, then went over it with a deep black/brown artist's oil wash, and outlined each area to represent the layer of paint. This gave the paint depth and dimension.

13 I laid hobby plywood in the truck bed, painted it flesh, overcoated it with burnt umber artist's oil, and let it sit for 15 minutes.

14 After 15 minutes, I loaded a No. 6 flat brush with thinner, dabbed off most of the thinner with a paper towel, and used linear strokes to remove the burnt umber oil in streaks to replicate wood grain. The tape kept the burnt umber from getting all over the inside of the vehicle.

15

Next, I overcoated the wood grain with a thin mix of Tamiya flat brown (XF-10), flat black, and 80 percent thinner to soak up some of the oils and lighten the effect.

16

To create different depths of color that show different layers of the wood, I scuffed and removed some of the paint using alcohol. The alcohol removed the acrylics but didn't hurt the oils underneath, so the grain stayed in place.

18

I made a Toyota stencil to letter the back of the technical. (These days, as easy as it is to print decals, I would have done this differently.) I designed the lettering in Adobe Photoshop, measured it, printed it out on heavy-stock paper, and cut it out. I painted the stencil first so I could see it better.

17

Up front, on the hood, I highlighted some of the metal with bright silver to get a more three-dimensional look to let different amounts of metal show through, such as where the bolts rubbed through the hinges.

19

To protect the vehicle, I used 3M low-tack painter's tape. I like the tape to have even less tack, so I put it on my T-shirt and ripped it off a few times to take off more adhesive. Otherwise, it would take the paint right off the resin surface. On the inside of the A, I had to use a little bit of rubber cement to seal the stencil and prevent overspray.

20

After I removed the stencil, there was a little overspray, but after weathering it, the overspray was unnoticeable. I also touched up things here and there with the base color.

21

I painted the front grille and then added some rust to make it look properly damaged. That's an MV Products lens for the headlight. I put a bright bit of paint on the cable in the missing headlight to make that stand out. The bright rust on the fender is India red artist's oil.

22

On the rear tailgate, I used the base color for the chips. Inside the truck bed, you can see a mixture of Mig pigments climbing up the walls of the bed.

23

I built up more pigment in the back end, and you can really see the dimensional aspect of the paint on the hood. To weather the tires, I applied a base coat of flat black. Then I added oils, starting with a light tan wash.

24

On the tires, another very thin airbrushing of flat black homogenized the paint treatments, cleaned it up somewhat, and pulled everything together. A dusting of Dullcote clear flat toned down the headlight and added a dusty look to it.

25

That tailgate is rusting fast! If you look closely, you may notice a subtle drop shadow on the inside of the middle O. I did it on that letter to center your focus. It also gives the illusion of a slightly raised, stamped metal lettering, like the Toyota logo.

26 Oh, the brutality of weathering! This is an example of weathering to the extreme.

27 I was close to finishing the vehicle. From this distance, you get a good look at the rifle barrel and the fabric seat cover. However…

28 …the seat covers are not molded. I painted them to represent fabric. The painting produced that 3-D effect. I brush-painted Vallejo deck tan and added highlights and creases. On the floor, you can see more of my resin-cast ammo boxes.

29 Notice the highlight on the sidewalls. You'll see a lighter gray highlight painted between the tread pattern and the sidewalls that adds depth and dimension. I dirtied the fender wells with airbrushing and a No. 6 flat brush dipped in thinned artist's oils. I wiped most of the paint off with a paper towel, pulled back the bristles with my fingers, and let it fly! That's the mud speckling around the fender.

30 I used Citadel acrylic brass and copper to paint the machine-gun bullets. Citadel paints are popular with modelers who paint gaming figures—and they're some of the best metallics out there.

31 The dashboard dials were brush-painted and highlights added to the steering wheel and gun barrel. On the breech, I brush-painted the lighter gray areas to show scratches and chips. The barrel was painted flat black and then Tamiya clear blue and smoke.

Congolese Type 69 hybrid

Tamiya's 1/35 scale Soviet T-55 tank, like its full-size counterpart, is the starting point for endless variants. Here, a Type 69 hybrid is manned by members of the 1st Armored Brigade of the Democratic Republic of Congo.

The maelstrom of war has been raging in the Congo for decades. The tank I modeled here is a Type 69, a Chinese-built variant of the Soviet T-55. It belongs to the Democratic Republic of Congo's 1st Armored Brigade. My model is but a tiny microcosm of a war so jumbled it was difficult to tell who the belligerents were or even what side they were fighting on. For example, the 1/35 scale Tamiya T-55 model I began with was converted to a Chinese Type 69, but it incorporates elements that might have been manufactured in Russia, China, Eastern Europe, or elsewhere.

1 The olive plastic is Tamiya's T-55. The conversion to a T-69 occurs by installing different running gear and details, mainly the taffy-colored resin parts, from Verlinden's Type 69 conversion set (No. 2655) with Trakz road wheels. On the glacis plate, white strips of styrene fill unused locator holes where T-55 details would have gone.

2 Texturing the turret gives it a roughcast, realistic look, but the resin doesn't come that way. To achieve this, I coat the surface with liquid cement and then cover it with fine silica sand. The taffy-colored resin details are added after the texture dried. The shiny cupola on the left is a plastic part from my spares. Brass and copper wire replicate tie-down bars and electrical conduit, respectively. White styrene plugs unused locator holes.

3 White styrene strips and plugs fill locators on the back as well. The tie-downs on the side of the turret are copper wire, photoetched-metal mesh goes over the engine deck, and the stowage box on the back of the turret is from the kit.

4 More detail made from snippets of wire are visible from above. In addition to the copper tie-downs, solder wire and a scrap of styrene replicate conduit running to the laser rangefinder at the top of the mantlet. Thicker solder wire represents the fuel lines between the tanks on the right fender. A wire with insulation left on part of it hangs loose at the rear of the turret, hinting at a missing formation light. The drainage holes in the fenders are built-in standard features. Otherwise the fenders would rust off.

And that's why this tank looks like it does—and says what it says about a place where the deadly business of war became a way of life. I wanted this tank to represent evil. You're talking about a Third World war, a vicious campaign. The skull and cross-bones imagery has been used in the Congo for years by mercenaries. While research-ing, I saw photos of it on several different vehicles, so I replicated it. The real tank had

a vehicle number of 91; I added another 1 (9/11) to express the presence of terror.

Converting the tank

I started with Tamiya's 1/35 scale T-55 (kit No. 35257) base model—what you see in olive, **1**. The taffy-colored resin parts were mostly from Verlinden's Type 69 conver-sion set (No. 2655), and the wheels were made by Trakz.

The turret has a roughcast texture that was created by brushing liquid cement on the turret and coating it with silica sand, which has an especially fine grain, **2**. On the turret, the base of the commander's hatch came from my spares box. I used .020" brass wire for grab handles, and ran copper wire from the driver's periscopes.

I also used copper wire for tie-downs on the back of the turret (a much better

5

I check the figure poses often during the build to make sure the soldiers fit in naturally with their surroundings. If the figures are painted with acrylics, as these are, I can apply heat to manipulate an arm or leg as needed without damaging the paint. If the figures are painted with oil, it would be more risky.

6

To paint a darker complexion, I overcoat a burnt umber base coat with sienna orange for highlights. Then, a finish coat of flesh blends the previous two coats and leaves highlights in relief.

7

The skulls are resin castings from Warriors. I hollowed them out with a motor tool, which was no mean feat. I lost several of them before I was through adding them to the antenna.

8

Friulmodel metal tracks are on and their sag is set. The tracks come out of the box as bright metal, which I tone down with rail-weathering solution.

representation than the flat, two-dimensional pieces found in detail sets of photoetched metal), **3**. As I replaced details of the T-55 with items specific to the Type 69, I continued to fill the unused locator holes with bits of white styrene, such as where T-55 fuel drums would go. The screen on the engine cooling fans was photoetched metal from Verlinden, and the antenna base was also a Verlinden part.

On top of the turret, I used solder wire to replicate wiring for the laser-designated rangefinder on the mantlet, **4**. I also added strip styrene ribs to the top of the barrel where the thermal sleeves are joined. At the rear top of the turret, I added wire with some of the insulation left on it. That would have been a formation light, but now it's battle damage.

On the right side of the hull, I added

fuel cells from my spares box, and joined them with solder wire as fuel lines. The formed brass on the right fender represents a tow-cable bracket. On the port side, up by the headlights, I used a strip of styrene for a headlight mount. And what do you know? The stowage box on the rear was actually from the Tamiya kit.

Now, we are beginning to see what makes this tank a hybrid. For example, that big box on the back of the turret is characteristic of the Czech version of the tank. Then there are unmatched cupolas. The small one on the port side, with the light on it, is a standard loader's cupola. However, the cupola on the right side, where the machine gun is, is a ballistic cupola usually found on a different version of the T-55. So this hybrid is just a bunch of parts from different tanks that

were thrown together. It's a mash-up.

Before adding too many more details, I wanted to test-fit the figures, **5**. The figures were from Warriors that I painted years ago and kept around for the day I would need them. Now, their time had come, and I made sure their poses looked natural with the equipment around them. To paint darker skin tones, I went with a dark color and added sienna orange for highlights. Adding a flesh tone blended the highlights and made the features pop, **6**.

At the front of the tank, I installed a grisly addition to the antenna, **7**. Yes, those are skulls, and I saw various research photos that showed this detail on tanks. The skulls were a resin product from Warriors. And to tell the truth, they were a real pain! I hollowed them out with a motor tool and lost three or four

9

Installing these Friulmodel tracks is not necessarily the easy way, but there's no substitute for the look and heft of real metal. As the weathering solution settles into the tracks, it defines details and lends more realism.

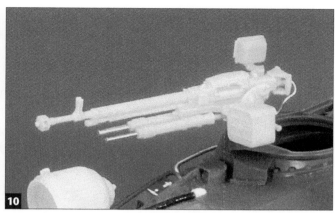

10

The DShK machine gun is a Soviet-made weapon sometimes called *Dushka* (Russian for *Sweetie*). This little darling is a resin piece from Blast Models. Note the solder wire used for the fire-control cable.

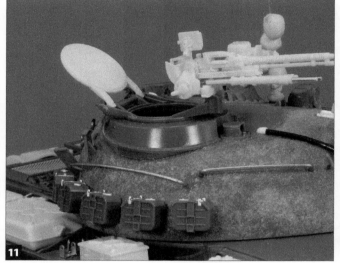

11

I add bits of styrene to the ammo cans. These are mounting clips, a detail not seen on this or any other commercially available moldings. For a reference, I have one of the "real McCoys," an ammo can a friend brought back from Afghanistan, where similar tanks are found.

12

Here, the tank's base coat has been applied with Tamiya paints: Tamiya black green (XF-59) with a little bit of dark green (XF-61). I also fit the tank in position on its base. Note how the turret is positioned.

of them in the process. Even at a slow speed, the motor-tool bit would catch a little and zing! they'd be flung across the room and lost forever. They were hard to hold onto, and you can't use pliers because you'll mash them. So I had to hold them with my fingers, and run the motor tool at low speed, with a variable-speed foot control. Still, every once in a while the grinding burr would grab and toss them or, worse yet, jump and rip across my finger.

I must have test-fit the skulls a dozen or more times before I got them positioned how I wanted. That's why I took the photo at this point; I just wanted to

make sure of how they looked. Eventually, I set their poses, and numbered them 1 through 4 to keep track of them. I painted each one a little differently.

Adding tracks and more details

I installed the Friulmodel tracks on the tank and set the sag, **8**. I always test-fit the tracks before painting them to make sure they have the proper fit and sag. These tracks are made of metal, kind of expensive, and sometimes difficult to assemble and install. But armor modelers (*tread heads*, as they're sometimes called) all agree that nothing looks more like metal than metal.

Right out of the box, the metal tracks were bright and shiny. But I applied a wash, so they were a hazy gray. For this wash, I used Micro Engineering rail weathering solution, a model railroad product that's perfect for this application. Photo **9** shows how the weathering solution built up in the links of the track. It's a gradual process that produces a realistic look for the tracks.

The same can be said for detailing in general. Most of it is not terribly difficult, but realism is cumulative. I used my motor tool to beat up the fenders, which added a little life to the model. Those fenders have got to be beat up. You'll never see a picture of them in any other condition.

13

14

A dusting of a highlight coat, a lightened shade of the base coat, hits the high spots and contrasts them with recesses and shadowy areas to bring detail into greater relief.

A darker shade, selectively airbrushed into shadowy areas and recessed details, turns up the contrast and replicates the effect of light and shadow on objects.

Realistic detailing can be easy to see, as on the fenders, or more subtle, such as the brass wire I added to the machine gun, **10**, or the extra details (bits of white styrene) added to the ammo cans on the lower right of the turret, **11**. Another such detail is electrical wire representing a conduit to the searchlight cable. Again, there's always something a little different in each new look as the build progresses.

15

The sum of the details on the tank, plus the modeling of the figures, adds up to an evocative vignette from the terrible conflict in the Congo.

Painting and decals

Finally, it was time to paint the tank. I began by airbrushing the base coat of Tamiya black green with a little dark green mixed in, **12**. Next, I applied a lighter shade of the base coat to bring out details. As I painted the tank, I constantly checked the model on its base. I displayed this tank as more of a showcase piece. It rests on a modeled area of terrain attached to a wooden base, which is labeled "Type-69 Hybrid."

I added more shadows with a darker shade, then really turned up the contrast with another, even lighter shade of the highlight coat, **13**. You can really see it on the turret, fuel cells, and fenders. It's a good example of how paint can define shapes and emphasize details.

After I finished painting the tank, I added the decals. If you look to the right of the tank in photo **14**, you'll see a sheet of styrene, a test area, with some airbrushing and a decal. I designed the decal and had it printed on an ALPS

printer, which can print in white. (I could have also outlined it and printed it on white decal sheet, but this was easier.) I tested the decal on the styrene with paint that had not been sealed to make sure that the decals were compatible with the finish and that they were going to stick.

On the turret, I wet the area where the decal goes with Pledge Future floor polish. I applied the Future and floated the decal into it. Then I gently pushed the decal into the heavily textured surface with a soft cloth, and applied Solvaset decal solution, which softened the decal so it conformed to the surface underneath it. I repeated

this step and made sure there were no air bubbles left under the decal, and then overcoated it with Future again. When the air bubbles were gone, the decal appeared to have been painted on instead of looking like a decal.

To place the tank number decal, I had to remove one of the ammo cans and the grab handles. It's much easier to get the decals set without obstructions and reattach details.

With the decals in place, the Type 69 hybrid tank of the Democratic Republic of Congo's 1st Armored Brigade was completed and ready for display on its base, **15**.

As a kid, and even after I got out of the Army, a TV tray was my workbench. For tools, I'd use my mom's tweezers and maybe a razor blade.

Now, I have a lot of tools in my workshop: a table saw, 6" sanders, a drill press, bending tools for metals and plastic, track jigs, plus various clamps and files.

The tools shown here are the ones I use the most. They are always on my desk. I've had many of them for 20 years or more (replacing blades and such). They're my old standbys. Everyone should use the tools that suit them best.

Also use what you can afford. I acquired most of these tools on the cheap, and I use them all the time. Spend money on special items. The first tool I felt like I spent money on was a Foredom motor tool. They are expensive, $300 or $400, but I burned out a Dremel and I had to have something. It gives me a lot of control, it runs as slow I want it to, and the foot pedal makes it even easier to work. It's deluxe, and it's been worth it.

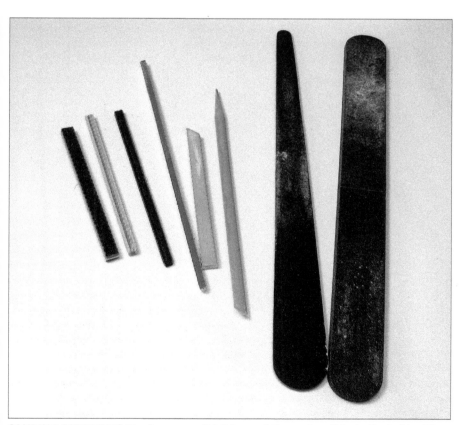

SANDING APPARATUS: You know, we didn't have all these nice sticks in the hobby 30 years ago. I like to buy a big bag of assorted sanding sticks, pads, and file sticks—I get them in a 40-count bag, all shapes and sizes. They're all different grits and thicknesses, and you can cut them to shape. The blue one with the point is great for getting into wrinkles and folds on figure uniforms. Be careful with metal files. They are too abrasive; if you don't know how to use one, you can make something lopsided in a hurry.

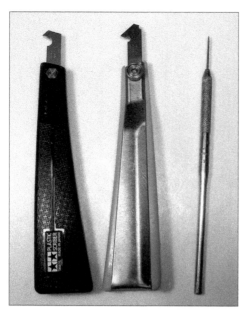

SCRIBING TOOLS: The yellow and the black ones are for cutting sheet plastic and plaster. Then I have a whole variety of dental tools with special points, such as the former dental pick on the right. It was a lot longer. I cut it off and ground it down to that point on the end. I use it for everything! (Believe it or not, my dentist supplies me with tools when I ask him.)

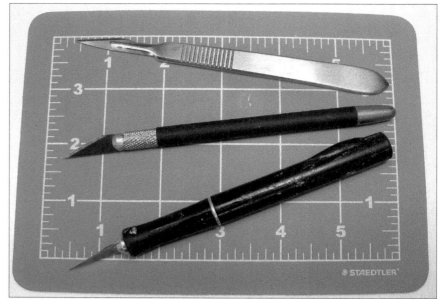

CUTTING TOOLS: I may have four work areas going at once, and I'll have knives like this at each station. I bought a bunch of cutting pads in a clearance sale, but usually I like having a glass working surface. At the top is a scalpel—it must be at least 20 times sharper than the average hobby knife. They're vicious! I use them occasionally when I'm working on a figure for very fine work, such as carving an eyeball. In the center is a No. 11 blade in a nice Staedtler Mars handle. At the bottom is a heavy-duty X-acto X2000, non-rolling handle, my go-to knife for most of my work. I like its heft and balance, and you can feel the weight of the knife in your hand as you cut and carve. I usually have it and the Staedtler Mars ready to go at my desk.

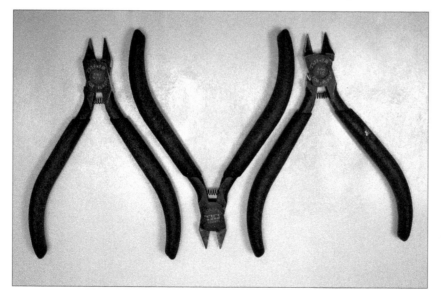

SIDE CUTTERS: These are Tamiya sharp-pointed side cutters. I go through these like candy. This is the best cutting tool in the world. I keep a bunch of them on hand because I'll use one for a short while and then demote it to being a secondary cutter. They're perfect for cutting plastic or resin, but don't use them on anything else if you want them to stay sharp. I have a cheaper cutter I can use on brass, and I have regular wire cutters or tinsnips for cutting piano wire.

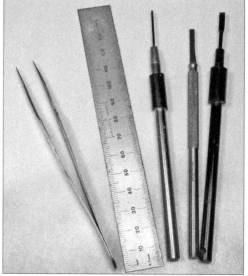

TOOL ASSORTMENT 1: At left is a nice, sharp-pointed tweezers. I use them for decals and placing small details on a model. Next is a machinist's rule, a stiff straightedge. It reads millimeters and inches on both sides. To the right of that is a Tristar micro chisel, which is great for getting into small places, but you have to use it carefully as it's very sharp. Next is a chisel-bladed scalpel from Micro-Mark. On the far right is a heavy-duty Tristar chisel.

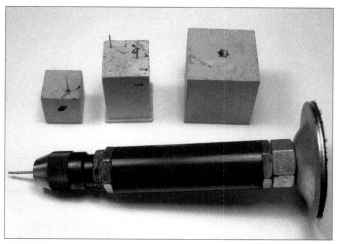

MICROSAWS: This is my assortment of photoetched-metal microsaws. They're handheld and flexible. They come in a range of thicknesses from .005"—very fine—to .010". They're not cheap, but I consider them a must-have. All the different shapes are useful for all kinds of models. The curved ones are especially handy for aircraft modelers who work around complex curves.

MOUNTING BLOCKS AND PAINTING STAND: When I have a figure to paint, I drill a hole in the bottom of it, stick a brass rod in there, and mount it to a temporary base. I can grab that base and hold it for painting. The largest block is tapped out for a screw that would hold bigger parts. I can tighten them down. In the foreground is a custom-made painting stand. It's a section of PVC with a drill chuck at the top and a very heavy base. I can mount figures on that rod, and the bottom swivels.

TOOL ASSORTMENT 2: The razor blade gets used for everything. With it, you can shave away unwanted details on a model and not displace much plastic. Below that is a mini tube cutter. I don't saw metal or styrene tubing—I use this Superior Tool Pro Line Mini Tubing Cutter. There are other brands, but this is a little heftier: It cuts from ⅛" to ⅞". Save your saw. Next to that is a machinist's square, which is indestructible. Measure twice, cut once. I use it to make square cuts on sheet styrene or to true up buildings on a diorama. The ball peen hammer here has interchangeable heads; I mainly use it with my punch-and-die set to knock out discs and rivets. At the far right is an adjustable pliers that is one of my most important painting tools, as it locks onto caps that are stuck on bottles.

MARKERS: I always keep markers around. On the left is a Copic Multiliner. It has a line weight of .05 and draws the finest line I've ever seen. And it's permanent. I use it a lot for marking and drawing when I scratchbuild. I also use it for nose art, name tags, and lettering on tanks and aircraft. For making a name tag, I use this to create the outline and then color it in. In the center is a fine-point Sharpie; I use this for a lot of the same purposes as the Multiliner, but it's not as fine. And then there's the big fat Sharpie. I use that more than any of the others, mainly for labeling things. I don't use pencils much, except for marking wood (to prevent ink from soaking into the wood).

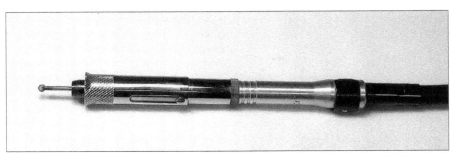

MOTOR TOOL: This is the business end of a Foredom flexible-shaft motor tool. I have a round grinding burr chucked into it here. The tool is run by a foot pedal. Foredom makes these tools for dentistry and other applications; this one is from a jeweler's set. It's a very smooth, variable-speed tool.

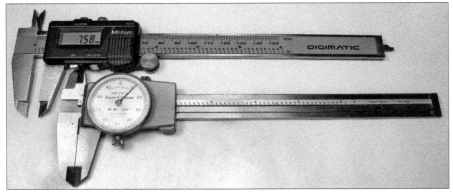

CALIPERS: A caliper is an essential scratchbuilding tool—I swear by it. I have micrometers, too, but I rarely use them. These are both nice, high-end instruments. You get what you pay for. Sometimes you can find great deals at a show, but, generally, if you want high quality you have to pay well. The digital caliper displays inches or millimeters, but the other one, a mechanical one, needs no battery.

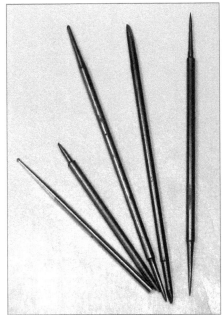

MICRO TOOLS: The first tool on the left is a micro burnishing tool. I use it to rub down dry transfers. The other four are custom-made micro sculpting tools. I had seen modelers carve toothpicks into certain shapes, harden them with super glue, and turn them into very specific tools for sculpting putty. I had some like that, but then a friend offered to turn brass rods on a lathe to the same shapes. These brass tools are very durable.

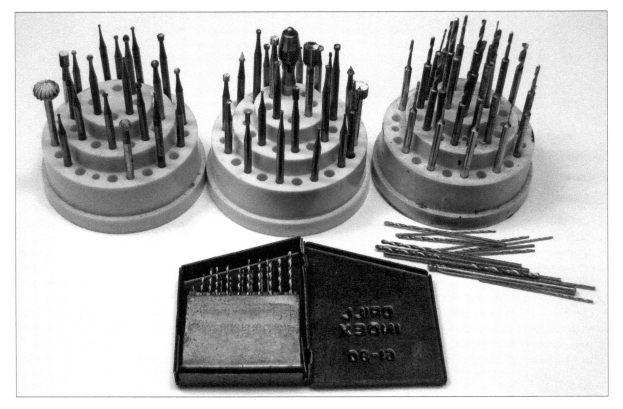

DRILL AND MOTOR-TOOL BITS: The larger ones go in my Foredom motor tool. The others, such as the micro bits in the black box, go in a pinvise. So I have all shapes and sizes, with bits up to 1". (By the time I go that big I'm using a variable-speed drill.)

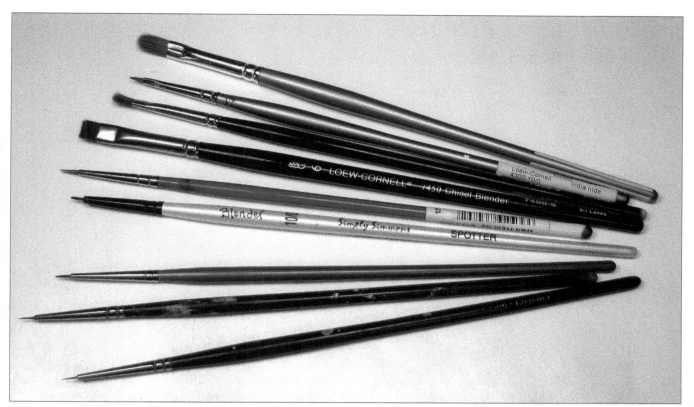

STANDARD PAINTBRUSH ASSORTMENT: Here is my standard assortment of paintbrushes. I can paint everything and anything with these. People will preach about paintbrushes, but you don't have to spend a fortune on them; all but two of these are from a craft store. I will buy Winsor & Newton Series 7 brushes for top performance, and those are pretty expensive—about five times more than any of the other brushes! On the two brushes at the bottom, I've taken a razor and cut most of the bristles out of them to make them even finer. They come in handy for painting eyebrows and other tiny details.

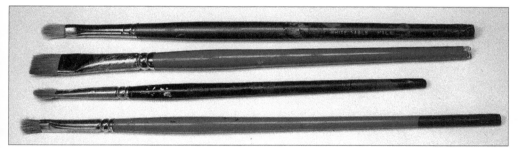

JUNK BRUSHES: These brushes look pretty rough for a good reason—they are! But I wanted you to get a good look at the stuff I actually use. These are my larger brushes, which I use for groundwork, dry-brushing, and large-area work. The brush at the bottom is starting to look pretty fuzzy, and I use it for stippling groundwork and clays. Notice that I've chopped the handles off of several brushes. I like to choke up on them, and a long handle just gets in the way and knocks things over—so I cut them down. The red brushes are Winsor & Newton. From the top, you'll see a No. 4 Filbert, a No. 2 flat, another No. 4 Filbert, and then what's left of a Filbert. As my good brushes get used, I cycle them out, so I always have a junker handy for the rough work.

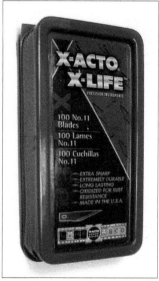

HOBBY KNIFE BLADES: I do use regular No. 11 blades, but when you need the very best, keenest edge, these are fantastic blades. They are more flexible, extra sharp, and longer lasting. I ration them since they are expensive.

NO. 6 FILBERT: My go-to No. 6 Filbert brush is a Cornell No. 4500. I like the Filbert style because it tapers. So when you dry-brush and angle the brush, there's paint in it all the way across so the paint gets evenly distributed. I load it, wipe it off, and everything at the top has paint. I use it for everything.

CHISEL BLENDER: I don't actually use this Cornell No. 6 chisel blender for blending. I like to use it for applying paint. This nice, sharp flat brush is great on edges and in corners.

FINE-POINT BRUSH: Winsor & Newton Series 7 No. 000 fine-point sable is the finest brush I have. I've even cut off some of the bristles to make it finer and taper the tip a little more.

RAZOR SAW BLADE: That's a good ol' razor saw blade! I use it for cutting wood, plastic, and larger stuff. I do not like using the wood handle that comes with it; they're too flexible and not rigid enough for me, so I hold the blade in my hand when I cut. That's a little risky. You obviously have to be careful not to cut yourself. But I like the control much better.

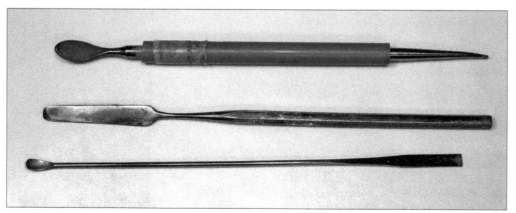

PUTTY AND PAINT TOOLS: At the top is a dental tool for mixing putty. (One end's broken off, so I got it for free.) I use it for scooping paint pigment from the bottom of containers. Below that is a palette tool, another dental item. Dentists use it for mixing putties; I use it for mixing artist's oils as well as putty. At the bottom is a Tamiya paint stirrer, with a little spoon on one end and a flat end on the other.

MICRO SCALPEL: This is a micro scalpel with a chisel blade, which is available from Micro-Mark. And believe me when I tell you it is a scalpel—it will go through your finger, no problem. It is sharper than a razor blade. I use it very cautiously for the finest of details to sculpt, carve, or remove the tiniest bits.

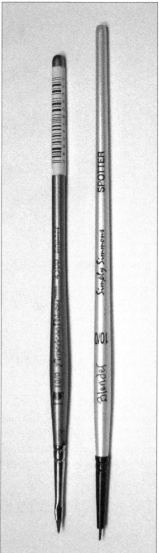

BLENDERS: At left is a 10/0 fine blender. This mini Filbert brush is what you blend oils with. You get in there and you dab two colors together—you don't have to get in there and stir it around, you just dab those two colors where they come together, and it blends them. At the right is a Robert Simmons (Simply Simmons) spotter. Notice on the handle I wrote *Blender*. I wanted to make sure I marked it. What I did was cut back the tip, so I have those bristles going straight to a nice, round tip—not a point. That's my micro blender for really small areas, like 1/35 scale cheeks and chins.

PUNCH-AND-DIE SETS: These are my punch-and-die sets, which are essential to scratchbuilding and detailing. I have three round sets, plus an old hexagonal set that used to be sold by Historex Agents from Great Britain.

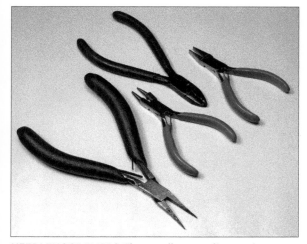

NEEDLENOSE PLIERS: The needlenose pliers at the bottom are my fave. I use these flat and pointy pliers for bending photoetched metal and brass wire. The round-headed micro pliers is handy for forming wire; the flatnose micro pliers for shaping or folding photoetched metal. I use the side cutters at the top to cut brass on electronic circuit boards. (I've had that tool for 30 years!)

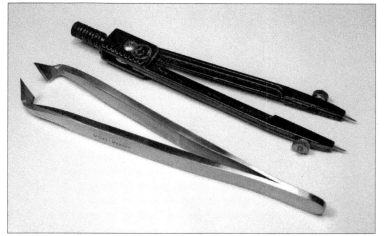

DIVIDERS AND TWEEZER CUTTERS: At the top, dividers, and below that, the sharpest tweezer cutters in the world. I get those from Jon Vojtech at UMM-USA. They are absolutely the best for removing a part from a tight spot on the sprue.

Scott Primeau, from Minneapolis, painted this 75mm (1/25 scale) Knight Models figure: U.S. Special Forces, Afghanistan. I liked it so much I bought it. The grittiness of the character fits a soldier with the call sign "Cowboy," one of the early guys in Afghanistan. Scott's eye for color shows in the detail and skin tones. He nailed the colors of the uniform, and it's a tricky one to do. Right down to the dust on the weapon, the whole thing has the essence of a miniature in combat.

This is an M5A1 Stuart tank in Normandy, 1944, by John Rosengrant. It's the 1/35 scale AFV Club kit with resin upgrades from Tiger Models. John scratchbuilt the Culin hedgerow cutter on the front of the tank from styrene strip. He base-coated the tank in Tamiya olive drab and used various shades of Lifecolor paints for highlighting and weathering. The figures are scratchbuilt and painted mostly with Vallejo acrylics. The diorama was inspired by pictures from the fight for St. Lô in Normandy in July 1944. In looking at the composition of the scene, nothing is square with the base; there are no right angles. The wall and the soldiers aboard the tank break the horizontal plane, and the nose of the tank and the soldier leaning out break the edges, yet the tank's gun barrel draws your eye back into the scene. *John Rosengrant*

John Rosengrant shows a master's touch with this diorama featuring Dragon's 1/35 scale Panther Ausf A. He added an Aber barrel and photoetched-metal details and put the tank on Modelkasten tracks. Zimmerit, the antimagnetic paste Germans put on tanks to thwart magnetic mines or "sticky bombs," comes in resin sheets from Atak. John used Lifecolor paints on the Panther with details in Vallejo paints. Mig pigments provide most of the dust and weathering accents. The figures are all scratchbuilt, and he painted them with Vallejo acrylics. Inspiration for the diorama came from a famous photograph of a 12th SS *Hitlerjugend* Panther and panzer grenadiers near Norrey-en-Bessin early in the fight for Normandy. The building is a MK35 Editions plaster building modified to more closely resemble the one in the photograph. John scanned his reference photo and used Adobe Photoshop to design a large dry transfer for the St. Rémy advertisement on the wall; weathering blended it in. *John Rosengrant*

Dragon LVT(A)-1 Alligator, 1/72 scale by Bob Bethea, Austin, Texas. For 30 years, he's taught me a lot of modeling tricks, like how to use Future floor polish. The vibrance of the piece really stands out, the blue/green of the water, the sand for contrast, the markings on the amtrac, everything pops.

This is a favorite of mine from an AMPS (Armor Modeling and Preservation Society) show a few years ago was by Ron Domatrowski, of Chicago. It's AFV Club's 1/35 scale M35A2 2½-ton cargo truck (kit No. AF35004), heavily distressed to depict a Somali technical. The figure is from a Warriors Scale Models African tankers set; the gun mounted on the truck bed is from Eastern Express. It's a nice piece of kitbashing on a simple, effective base.

Japanese modeler Masaya Saito used an old 1/32 scale Airfix kit to build a hypothetical Bentley, a "what-if" SAS scout car. The No. 8 near the spare tires, is left over from the car's former career as a racer. The figures are all converted and built from bits of spares or scratchbuilt pieces. *Masaya Saito*

Acknowledgments

I would like to thanks the following modelers, artists, and friends who have been a great influence on me and my modeling capabilities over the past 40 years:

Robert "Uncle Bob" Bethea
Stephen Burrus
Mike Good
Dieter Mattingly
Dave Mosser
Mike O'Connor
Jaume Ortiz Forns and Masahiro Doi
Shepard Paine
John Rosengrant
Stephen "Cookie" Sewell
Brian Stewart
John Stonesypher (The Grenadier Shop)
François Verlinden
Ron Volstad
Harold "Hap" Wolfgram

I would also like to thank the following people and organizations for their support and contribution in the production of this publication:

At the Front/Rollin Curtis
Mirko Bayerl/Toni Canfora
Robert Bethea
Sam Brister
Bronco Models
Pearce Browning (Miniatures PMC)
Canon Camera
Dan Capuano
Greg Cihlar
Fletcher Clement
Alexander De Leon
Ron Domatrowski
Robert Döpp
Marco Fernandez
Iain Hamilton
Mark Hembree
Ben Jakobsen
Mig Jimenez (AMMO of Mig Jimenez)
Kalmbach Publishing
Michael Knott (M.P.K. Enterprises)
Douglas Lee
Mike Littlefield (Harder & Steenbeck)
David Manter
Chris Merseal (CRM Hobbies)
Marcus Nicholls (Tamiya Publications)
Yaroslav Padalko (Live Resin)
Alan Presley (Big Al's Bases)
Scott Primeau
Charlie Pritchett
Reaper Miniatures/Paint
Frank Rincon (Uniform & Equipment Advisor)
Cesar "Manny" Rodriguez
John Rosengrant
St. Louis Cardinals
Masaya Saito
Ken Schlotfeld (Badger Airbrush)
Carlos Startin
Tamiya
Vallejo Paints
Ron Volstad (Volstad Historical Art)
Harold "Hap" Wolfgram

A special thanks goes out to members of the U.S. Armed Forces.

And I'd especially like to thank my wife Nancy Mrosko, who has had to deal with me and my attitude and shenanigans for the past 14 years.

This illustration of Chris is by Ron Volstad, noted for his graphics in books and on model kit boxes. It shows Chris during his days in the U.S. Army.

B orn and raised in Springfield, Ill., Chris Mrosko has succeeded in living the dream of many avid hobbyists—finding a way to make his passion his livelihood.

As an artist and designer, he has worked with well-known hobby manufacturers, such as Custom Dioramics, Miniatures PMC, W Britain Miniatures, VLS Corp., and the Warriors and New World Miniatures lines of scale figures, creating buildings and display bases as well as sculpting original masters for figures.

Like other kids in the 1960s, he built trendy plastic models like Revell's Dune Buggy. He was lured to dioramas by reading the booklets that came with Monogram kits, and after seeing built-up dioramas at a local hobby shop, he was hooked.

Following a three-year hitch in the U.S. Army, he continued to improve his modeling skills while working in the museum of the 2nd Armored Division. He turned completely pro in 1991, moving to California to take a position with what was then known as Dragon/Kirin.

It was there that he met John Rosengrant, a master modeler known for his character effects work in *Avatar, Jurassic Park, Terminator,* and other films. Together they formed Warriors Scale Models.

In 1999, Chris returned to his native Midwest, where he continues to make a living at his hobby—and living his dreams.

About the author

Lightning Source UK Ltd.
Milton Keynes UK
UKHW050708270721
387832UK00001B/7